ACHIEVING PEACE
OF HEART

by
Rev. Narciso Irala, S. J.

Xavier College
Managua, Nicaragua

TRANSLATED BY

LEWIS DELMAGE, S.J.
Saint Joseph's College
Philadelphia, Pa.

Dedicated to
the Sacred Heart of Jesus
and
the Immaculate Heart of Mary

St. Jerome Library
WWW.STJEROMELIBRARY.ORG

Copyright © 2019 St. Jerome Library Press
Elkhorn, Wisconsin

All rights reserved. No part of this book may be reproduced or transmitted in any form or by any means, electronic or mechanical, including photocopying, recording, or by any information storage or retrieval system, without written permission from the publisher.

Imprimi Potest:
> THOMAS E. HENNEBERRY, S.J.
> > *Praep. Prov. Neo-Ebor.*

Nihil Obstat:
> JOHN M. A. FEARNS, S.T.D.
> > *Censor Librorum*

Imprimatur:
> ✠ FRANCIS CARDINAL SPELLMAN, D.D.
> > *Archbishop of New York*

(The *nihil obstat* and *imprimatur* are official declarations that a book or pamphlet is free of doctrinal or moral error. No implication is contained therein that those who have granted the *nihil obstat* and *imprimatur* agree with the contents, opinions, or statements expressed.)

Translator's Introduction

FATHER IRALA'S ORIGINAL WORK, *O Contrôle Cerebral*, was first published at S. Paõlo, Brazil, in 1944. Shortly thereafter various foreign language translations appeared in Europe and Latin America and were as enthusiastically received as the original Portuguese edition. But until now the work was unavailable to English-speaking readers—an omission which the present authorized translation has finally remedied.

The need for such a book is readily apparent. All of us at one time or another experience what—in the jargon of the psychologist—are called "personality maladjustments." These may be and usually are minor mental disturbances of one kind or another—doubt, worry, fear, and so forth—which, while not always requiring the specialized (and expensive) services of a psychiatrist, need very much to be corrected and avoided. To this end we need a practical handbook or manual that will outline an effective method of procedure. This translation of Father Irala's work does, we feel, more than adequately fulfill that need.

However, a word of warning may not be out of

place at this point. Father Irala never intended this book as a panacea for all mental ills of whatever kind or degree. He does not pretend that the serious complications of a neurosis or psychosis admit of any facile solution to be found in the pages of this or any other manual. Special disorders must continue to require the attention of the specialist. But the ordinary, everyday problems of inefficiency, mental wandering, worry, overwork, insomnia, and loss of self-control, these he feels may be treated and an effective cure found for them in the manner here indicated.

The important thing is that Father Irala's methods have been found to work. His book is a manual of practice. It is meant, as the author himself says, not to be read on the run but to be studied and put into practise. Professional men who have read the manuscript—educators, guidance counsellors, and directors of souls—have already testified to its effectiveness. But even more impressive has been the testimony of those who have personally profited from the author's work. Many of these actual cases are detailed throughout the text; many more have been by word of mouth; many, finally, have come to the author in a steady stream of letters and correspondence from all over the world. People who have never met him but who have read his book in Spanish, Portuguese, Italian, or Polish, have written to ask his advice or to tell him how much he has helped them.

The author is, of course, a Catholic priest. His book is the product of years of experience both as a priest and as a practising psychologist. It is a book, therefore, written out of knowledge and charity, and as such it will prove equally valuable to all—regardless of religious belief—who take it up in an awareness of their own need and with a true desire for self-help. For surely they are not only Catholics who experience bouts of depression; the experience is universal and has universal implications. All man's dreams and daring, all the richness of his emotional and affective life, all this forms a unity with his rational activity. Intellect and will are not discarnate. The whole man acts, thinks, desires, loves, hopes and fears. All this human activity has been symbolized by the human heart—for, indeed, do we not say that a man is great-hearted, hard-hearted, chicken-hearted, weak-hearted? And for those who do believe, all man's ideals are symbolized and incarnate in the Heart of Christ. The peace of that Heart, which He would give to us, is there to be had, to be achieved. Father Irala outlines for us how many natural means, too, can help us to that supernatural goal.

Grateful acknowledgment is here made to the Rev. Charles J. Lewis, S.J. for his careful reading and checking of the entire manuscript, and to the Rev. Mark H. Bauer, S.J. for his advice on the use of biological and medical terms.

L. D.

To

*all who would direct
their feet in the way of peace of heart—*

THIS BOOK IS
EARNESTLY DEDICATED

Preface

THE DANGERS of the atomic age in which we live are outward signs of a still more terrible, because interior, explosive force. The mental life of modern man, his thoughts and impulses, his desires and feelings, his nervous breakdowns and chaotic hurrying and worrying, all these are more immediately threatening than atomic warfare.

Almost every week we discover new scientific, industrial, and political frontiers. We live in a day of atomic research, atomic explosions, atomic history. All the day long we are exposed to explosive impressions from newspapers, radio, TV and the movies; in travel we ride the protracted explosion of jet planes; and we frequently find our business and social life building up frantically to an explosive potential. Everywhere we seem to have a thousand harrying details to attend to, and we find it harder and harder to live within the framework of twenty-four hours. All this exerts a fearful pressure on our interior life, so great a pressure indeed that to many of us our personal lives seem little more than one minor explosion after another.

In our thinking we no longer have that Socratic

calm in which ideas follow one another in order. We have exchanged the Greek "sophrosyne" or classic poise for a ragged horde of images and ideas. We lack the peace we need to concentrate our attention on one individual idea. From this come confusion, mental fatigue, nervousness, uneasiness, insomnia, and the like.

In our feelings that moderation of our forefathers, as well as the healthy and holy gaiety of their family life, is yielding place to abnormal or incoherent impressions, precocious or even brutal impulses, and exaggerated fears or desires. These become ingrained or magnified, or transfer themselves to undue objects. They give rise to all kinds of unreasonable fears (phobias), obsessions, anxieties, worries and troubles.

In our decisions and goals we are no longer personalities with fixed norms to follow. Nor do we face the problems of life courageously and overcome its difficulties. On the contrary we find people without principles or strength of will, men and sometimes youths who are so disillusioned that they will even go to the extreme of committing suicide. They have a jumble of stray impulses and foolish desires which come from outside stimuli or unchecked instinct. These take the place of deliberate decision governed by reason and go on to produce indecision, loss of will power (abulia), inconstancy and discouragement. Finally the higher level of consciousness loses control of the impulses which come from its lower subconscious levels. And the will loses control over the drives toward mere sense pleasure.

Too frequently life turns out to be agitated and restless, amusing, if you will, but sad and empty, tormented, anarchical. For some it is living without knowledge of how to rest peacefully or work efficiently. For others it is ignorance of how to have a real desire, or how to dominate feelings or the sexual instinct. For many it is a life empty of interior happiness and, at least for some, merely a heap of diversions and pastimes.

This book has been written in the hope of alleviating in some part such burdens and to give some guidance in the re-education of control. It is primarily the fruit of the author's own personal experience.

In the first place it is meant for those who are fatigued from excessive work, worries or sufferings. Possibly they may have lost control of their thoughts and so will not know how to rest or sleep peacefully; or they may be unable to control their fears or sadness. The first part of the book is intended especially for this group.

Secondly, we are writing for those who are healthy of mind but who wish greater efficiency in studies or business, greater energy and constancy in carrying out plans, greater control of feelings or instincts, more joy, satisfaction and interior happiness. These will find useful and practical advice especially in the second part of the book.

Further, we are also writing for educators and

directors of souls who meet up with problem cases regarding study or virtue. These problems often arise because of mental wandering, inefficiency, indecision or even laziness of will. Difficulties may also come from uncontrolled passions, unreasonable fears, or feelings of inferiority.

In the arrangement of the book our purpose is, first of all, to be practical, to make it easier for you, our readers, to get quick control of your nervous and mental energies. The upshot of this will be greater efficiency in work and greater mental health. We want also to be accessible, even for non-specialists, in order to lessen mental sufferings and help those who need orientation or advice in their work or studies. We want, too, to save time for you. Hence we unify our teachings, condense explanations, make resumés of them and include outline diagrams or charts at the end of each chapter. We want, further, to focus your attention especially on mental fatigue, mental weakness, insufficient control and the internal difficulties which these cause. In practical applications we limit ourselves to the more immediate results of acquired control. And finally we want to interweave aphorisms or maxims which are educative and healthily optimistic. Once you engrave these on your mind by repetition, they will help to increase your health, efficiency and happiness.

Table of Contents

Translator's Introduction	5
Preface	9

Part I—RE-EDUCATION

Chapter

I.	Re-Education of Control	17
II.	Re-Education of the Mind	29
III.	Re-Education of the Will	53
IV.	Re-Education of the Feelings	67
V.	Resumé of Re-Educational Treatment	99

Part II—APPLICATIONS AND METHODS

VI.	How to Rest	113
VII.	How to Think	131
VIII.	How to Use the Will	145
IX.	How to Control Feelings	157
X.	How to Train the Sexual Instinct	185
XI.	How to Be Happy	194
XII.	How to Choose an Ideal	209
XIII.	A Short Summary of Advice	222

PART ONE

•

Re-Education

I

Re-Education of Control

As we point out in the outline diagram at the end of this chapter, there are definite symptoms of mental fatigue or weakness. The victim of fatigue or "overwork" almost always lacks clear and exact sensations. There is no unity or peace in his intellectual concentration. His will is undecided or wavering. His feelings or sense impressions are abnormally exaggerated. By re-education in the use of these four powers we can either cure him outright, or at least help him to cure himself.

If we do not all need this re-education, yet we can greatly profit by it. For feelings sometimes master us all. We are then sad and dispirited, bothered and impatient. We do not know how to control ourselves. We feel aversions and repugnances, attractions and inclinations which we should indeed control. But they drag us even further away from duty. "I am very sensitive, very nervous; I have too much feeling," we hear many say in order to defend or excuse their faults. They should really say, "I do not have much control of my sense impressions or feelings."

Now to govern feelings we must first control acts and ideas. The idea itself precedes and inclines us to the act. And acts and ideas both modify feelings. Like steam in the boiler of a locomotive, feelings are a chaotic force. Our ideas and will are the engineer who uses and directs it. So we must control those ideas. Now there are very many people who do not know what they are thinking about, or cannot think about what they wish, because they surrender to continued distractions in study, work and meditation. What unnecessary fatigue! What lost energy because of mental drifting and dallying! Yet they could perhaps be great inventors, artists, saints, if they would learn to concentrate their intellectual forces and will power upon an ideal. How many persons really want something? Perhaps they *think* they want something, but they do not carry out their plans because they make no real act of the will. They do not know how to use that sublime and immense force which we call "will power."

There are also many who do not know how to be happy, even in the lowest and most fundamental degree of enjoying mental rest in a good night's sleep. And when awake they have no concept of the tranquil and completely conscious sensations which could be theirs. These can be had by communicating with

RE-EDUCATION OF CONTROL [19

and possessing the objective goodness and beauty of the good God's external world.

Hence we shall explain how to re-educate and strengthen our receptive power through conscious sensations and voluntary acts. Relaxation and peace will be an automatic result. Then whether our thoughts are about things sensible or spiritual, concrete or abstract, we shall be masters of them. We shall be able to think when we wish and of what we wish, as well as withdraw our attention from what bothers or harms us. And this control of attention will be the means of re-educating our productive power.

When we can finally think freely of the good or the act we want to perform, we shall be able to desire it in earnest. Then we may pass easily and freely to its execution, even when under the influence of repugnance or subconscious fear.[1] In other words we shall have mental control, we shall become

---

[1] In speaking of the subconscious or subconsciousness in this practical manual we do not wish to plunge into philosophical distinctions, but merely to distinguish it from the conscious and from what is in practice liable to be confused with the unknown or unconscious.

A *conscious* mental phenomenon is known directly, concretely and experimentally. For instance, I am aware that I am joyful or that I hear music.

A *subconscious* one is known but not through direct experience. We can only reason to it. For instance, we reason to the existence of a tendency toward something from looking back on repeated acts.

An *unconscious* one is simply unknown; for example, some childhood fear, the cause of which still remains deep down and defies analysis.

again rational men, masters of ourselves, not slaves of irrational impulses.

At the end of this chapter there is an outline diagram of the symptoms, causes and remedies for fatigue or overwork. Pause here to take a preliminary glance at it. We do not pretend that our very short diagram explains *all* the symptoms, causes and cures for mental fatigue or weakness. Nor do we mean to set the boundaries of the physical and spiritual, which are so often glimpsed but confusedly. Our sole purpose in including this chart is to give a bird's-eye-view of the problem before beginning a further study of it.

To comprehend the chart better a good procedure will be to enter into the psychology of victims of the illness by listening to their own description of it. (Three case histories will shortly follow and more of them will be found throughout the book.) Unfortunately in the accelerated life of our age these victims are legion. They are recruited daily and not very often found among intellectual or affective nonentities. For these latter do not usually have the exuberance of mental life that is a prerequisite of swinging to an extreme and losing control. More often we see them among thinkers, writers and men of parts, among persons of exquisite sensibilities, among ambitious and talented students. How many lecturers, writers and professors of international fame have in our day been struck down by "overwork." Newton, for example, admitted that he could not work more than two hours a day. Even Dr. Vittoz, the psychiatrist, began by curing himself. And so it should not be a shameful or depressing thing to declare oneself mentally fatigued.

"At the age of twenty," a student describes himself, "despite an insatiable love of books, I suddenly found it impossible for me to study. Ten minutes of reading or writing brought on the most distressing feeling of fatigue. There was pain and, more frequently, a feeling of heat around the head and eyes. I simply could not drive off this sensation and concentrate on other ideas. A confusing succession of thoughts so oppressed me that I did not know how to control them. They were usually sad memories of the past, or painful anticipations of future misfortunes. They were sometimes so burdensome that I could not wholly drive them away by seeking refuge in conversation, walking or even manual labor. The most intimate part of my soul seemed split in two. I felt as if another part of me were overcoming the conscious part of me. Gradually I sank into discouragement, worry, feelings of inferiority and indecision. At times there was a swift transition from optimism to pessimism, from joy to sadness, without any objective cause. I was on an open road to all sorts of phobias, fear of appearing in public, incipient dizzy spells and scruples of conscience.

"A little later I fell prey to insomnia. My time of rest brought me no true repose. My sleep was interrupted by dreams and nightmares. When I got up I would find that I was more tired than when I went to bed. The illness and my sadness increased, yet those closest to me misunderstood it. When they saw me apparently strong and physically robust, some diagnosed that the illness came from my imagination. Others more charitably, but not more scientifically, tried to persuade me to do what I so anxiously wished to do, that is, not to be worried, not to be absent-minded, not to fear, to control myself. But they did not show me *how* to do it. It was as if you were to advise a person suffering from a fit of coughing or vomiting simply not to cough, not to vomit, without telling him the means to employ.

"I went through ten years of this. But after six months of exercises for mental re-education I triumphed over all those difficulties. Now I have almost forgotten that I had been ill. Although I have not yet recovered the same full capacity for work as heretofore, I do find that I am cured and satisfied."

I, too, the author, had to pass through that sorry state of distressing introspection. Yet it was useful. For my own pattern of mental activity was developed and illuminated first by the knowledge and advice of the famous Jesuit psychologist, Fr. Laburu.[1] It was afterwards completed and systematized in Lausanne by Dr. Arthus, according to the precepts of Dr. Vittoz.

They gave me the key to my cure in the re-education of control. This method I have confirmed by study and wide experience with the sick. It has taught me how to direct and console those who are

---

[1] Professor of Scientific Questions at the Gregorian University (Rome).

suffering from illnesses similar to mine. I say "to direct and console," for we should not prescind from medical aid. Even if symptoms seem to be alike, they sometimes have far deeper roots. In such cases only consultation with a spiritual psychiatrist could promise security and improvement.

"I am eighteen years old," a student once wrote to me, "and formerly I was strong as an oak. I could read for hours and hours without fatigue. I was very optimistic and felt capable of any undertaking. But last term I studied very little and had a lot of fun with various companions. As examination time drew near we spent several nights studying until three o'clock in the morning. We drove off sleepiness by means of coffee. But now that the examinations are over, I hardly know what has happened to me. Sleep is a torment. It is either a network of images or else a single image which continually repeats itself. Even during the day my head boils. I cannot pay attention to conversation. Reading tires me. I cannot distract myself. Life terrifies me; I am afraid of everything, even of myself."

This young man lost control because of excess and disorder in his mental work. Let such a one take heart, begin to strengthen his overexcited nervous system, perhaps travel a bit and rest. Then let him begin the work of mental re-education. He should start to form himself without waiting for somebody else to form and model him. See, for example, how children amuse themselves when they are alone. They build structures of clay or sand which they then enjoy leveling to the ground; so should we in solitude mold our characters and virtues, and destroy our defects.

Four everyday duties will help me to achieve a more healthy mental life. I must resolve, first, to strengthen and govern my body (nourishment, exercise and discipline); secondly, to feed and enlighten my intellect (serious, concentrated work); thirdly, to elevate and control my heart (love of God and neighbor); and finally, to strengthen and exercise my will (decision and constancy).

OUTLINE DIAGRAM

Mental Fatigue or Weakness

This fatigue or weakness is no mere imagination or fiction of the one who suffers from it. It is a true sickness, real and distressing. Usually it is not primarily organic but mental in origin. Those who have not experienced it find it hard to understand.

S	BODILY	Quite varied: a sensation of a band of heat or pressure around the head or forehead, a feeling of heaviness in the head, or headaches, nervous tension with little or no relaxation, nervousness both when awake and when desirous of sleep, waking at night and finding it impossible to go back to sleep, incipient dizziness, exaggerated or unaccountable rushes of blood to the face, difficulty in speaking in public, hypersensitivity of the sense of hearing, trouble with respiration, digestion, etc.
Y M P T O M S	In ideas or images	*Fixed ideas* (in general, depressing): discouragement, scruples, persecution complexes, phobias, etc.
		Currents of ideas (without being able to halt or channel them): associations imposed by the subconscious, impressions of the day which pass before the mind as if in a moving-picture, continual distractions, difficulty in fixing the attention, lessening or loss of memory.
	In consciousness (psychological, not moral)	Total or partial lack of clear consciousness and of adequate response to impressions. *Lack of objectivity*. The victim does not enter into reality or society but is engulfed in egocentrism. The victim does not live in or enjoy the present, does not attend to or obtain a clear notion of what he sees or hears. He lives in the past or future, far from the place where he is physically present, wrapped up in sadness, scruples, worries. A waking sleep. An exaggeratedly subjective life.
	In the affective faculties	Impressionability, excessive or persistent fears or desires. Emotional disorders. Anxieties. Alternating feelings of sadness or joy, peace or trouble, courage or discouragement, without an objective cause. The victim has lost control of his ideas and feelings.
	In the will	Indecision, loss of will power (abulia), instability, inconstancy. The victim acts on impulse, not by deliberation. As a consequence: a feeling of inferiority, helplessness and all kinds of phobias. He is a prisoner in a self-made prison-house.
	In short:	a bothersome duality and uncontrolled activity, loss of control and dominion over oneself.

BODILY CAUSES { (Sometimes efficient causes; in general, only predispositive): Heredity, malfunctioning of the endocrine glands, surgical trauma, organic depletion, nervous debility, excessive bodily fatigue.

MENTAL CAUSES {

Sudden: moral shock, convulsions (e.g., in bombardments).

Slow: come from a disordered psychical life:

a) in the *intellectual order*: work without periods of rest, or not rightly planned, or with two ideas. The parasite idea may be *impulsive*, such as an anxious pursuit of knowledge, business, virtue, prayer; in work, study, reading or prayer under pressure; e.g., trying to learn an hour's lesson in a few minutes. It may also be *depressive*: scruples, worry, discouragement, fear of fatigue, etc.

b) in the *affective order*: strong, uncontrolled impressions, anxiety, prudery, emotional conflicts which are repressed but not settled; family troubles; a bad education in modesty; continuous and accumulated impressions from novels and movies which in an hour make us live out the feelings of a whole year; a great disproportion between aspirations and possibilities.

c) in the *executive order*: intellectual or manual work with an urge to finish promptly (e.g., beginning a letter or business affair and already thinking of what is to come next; wanting to finish reading the whole newspaper in five minutes, etc.)

REMEDIES
{
BODILY: Physical education, sports, medicines, injections, shocks, electricity, etc. help to form an organism that is fit for the struggle or help to cure the organic part affected. They are onesided means. The great success of spiritual psychiatrists lies in their use of spiritual as well as bodily (somatic) means.

MENTAL:
a) *Passive*: The cure of rest, without giving the victim any occupation or distraction. Frequently this makes him worse. *Hypnosis* helps to investigate the subconscious, the roots of evil, and extirpate them. But it lends itself to abuse and leaves the victim more passive. Its effects are likewise obtainable by *suggestion*. This is good when in the hands of someone who knows how to induce it; sometimes it is difficult, but will be found easier in re-education. *Stimulation* can be private and personal, "I can do it, I shall overcome myself, I am not afraid." Or it can be collective (as used by spiritualists and similar types of religious believers). This is reducible to a suggestion, though not a very deep one.

b) *Active* (which do not necessarily exclude others): These are *auto-suggestion* and the *re-education* of mental control: re-education of sense consciousness, intellectual concentration, feelings and will. This is our system. Since the illness is above all a mental one, the cure must begin with the patient himself, with re-education and self-conquest.
}

II

Re-Education of the Mind

IN ORDER TO ATTAIN MENTAL mastery man should be capable of governing the kingdom of his mind, of opening or shutting its gates by receiving or rejecting thoughts at will. This mental activity is twofold: the mind receives sensations like a photographic camera or radio receiver, in which case the attention is gentle and almost passive; but it also produces images, ideas and reasoning processes like a movie projector or radio transmitter. Whether these are consciously or unconsciously elaborated, this is active or creative attention.

We base re-education upon the distinction between the receiving and producing powers of our mental world. Our axiom is that we cannot be fully both receiving and producing at the same time.

RECEPTIVE POWER

Receptive power is exercised when we receive conscious sensations. This means not only to stimulate our senses through noise, smells, hardness, and so forth, and to send nervous currents to our brain centers, but also to put more life into our sensations, receiving them consciously and filing them away in memory.

When distractions do not frustrate them from without and our secret thoughts do not tamper with them from within, conscious sensations are a tonic for the brain and the nervous system. They bring peace, joy, tranquillity and repose. They allow nature to work. Through them the objective world created by God enters within us with all its beauty. For if you know how to receive it within yourself you will obtain joy from the blue of the sky, peace of a starry night, beauty and variety of flowers, freshness of morning air, whisper of a fountain, whistling of wind, greenness of fields, trilling of birds, songs of innocent children.

Re-education of Receptive Power

Many persons rarely have clear sensations. This is especially true of the psychopathic or mentally ill. They live in their own subjective world which is sad and unreal. Only rarely do they come out into the exterior world, beautiful and joyful as it was created by God. And even when they do, their sensations are modified by extraneous or subjective thoughts. To these people we offer the following advice.

For your re-education you should apply your sense of sight for about ten or twenty seconds to a landscape, an object, a detail. Keep a tranquil or almost passive attention. Take your time. Consider the object before you and no other. Pay no attention to any other idea. Let the object enter within you as it is in itself, without any special effort. Look at it the way a young child does. Take care that the muscles of forehead and eyes are loose and relaxed. When your nerves and muscles are tense it is easy to have mental tension also. This results in lack of peace in the act of vision. But if your muscles relax your mind also tends to rest.

Apply your hearing to a near or distant noise. Let yourself be penetrated by the sound as above, naturally, without mental discussion of the fact or its cause. Be a mere receiver of sound and perceive it with pleasure and relaxation.

Apply touch by feeling objects, their coldness, heat, hardness and so on. Feel your own footsteps, the chair on which you are resting, the door opening. Feel your own breathing, the air entering your chest and filling it. The first sensation perceived will be the most conscious.

Walking Consciously.—This exercise is very useful for resting as well as for overcoming agoraphobia (that is, a morbid fear of crossing an open space or being out in the open). It also counteracts attacks of incipient dizziness. Hence we shall describe it in greater detail.

First get a separate sensation or clear consciousness of your foot being put down, your leg moving and your whole body sliding forward. Then co-ordinate these sensations and unite them to the rhythm of your breathing and to visual and auditory perception. You will then have a feeling of freedom and security.

Practising Conscious Sensations.—If you are haunted by this agoraphobia or by dizziness, exercise yourself in these sensations several times morning and afternoon. Do them, for example, on five different occasions. Each time spend about five minutes on them and receive five or more sensations through each sense.[1]

Try to experience, as far as possible, the truth in the old maxim, *"Age quod agis"*; that is, "Attend to what you are doing," or "Do what you're doing." But you must do all this as if in sport, with no anxiety, fear or worry.

In a few days you will notice a greater peace and joy. The world will appear more beautiful. It will, as a matter of fact, impress you as it really is in itself. It will not be colored by your uncontrolled unconsciousness.

A very depressed person once made this state-

---
[1] Follow the same norm in the concentration and will exercises. Do them the same number of times morning and afternoon. Each time do each exercise about five times in order to form a healthy habit.

ment to me: "After ten days of conscious sensations I feel myself another man. The world seems joyful and beautiful to me." Previously he had been looking at it through the prism of his sad thoughts. Or rather, he had been looking at it but had not seen it. Many people have been cured by this exercise alone.

Chinese painters, we are told, retire to a mountain before actually painting in order to contemplate and feel nature. They let it enter into themselves in all its beauty. Afterwards they transfer it to their canvas just as they sensed it. That is why their pictures have so much life and feeling. To allow exterior beauty to enter into oneself is characteristic of painters and poets.

PRODUCTIVE POWER

Under this heading we include ideas, images, associations of ideas and reasoning processes. These we produce voluntarily or they may be secretly produced by the unconscious. This "production" is active attention, work. This is the normal cause of fatigue which varies according to the kind of concentration.

Concentration

When we follow the course of one idea to the exclusion of every other, when we are attentive only to what we are studying or hearing and forget everything else, even ourselves, then the intellectual return is at its maximum. Then natural pleasure is great, and there is only that minimal fatigue which we call physical. Two hours of this perfect attention are equalized by five minutes of rest through conscious sensations ("receiving"). A day's work is balanced by a night's sleep. Thus we can work intensely at a single idea for many years, and intense and orderly study, far from weakening the brain, is a gymnastic which strengthens it.

Imperfect Attention.—Our attention is poor when we follow out one idea with another idea or image constantly interrupting it. This we call a distraction. Then the return and satisfaction are less and fatigue greater.

Our attention is harmful to us when we follow out several ideas simultaneously. This happens, for example, when we are reading or listening to an explanation or discourse and at the same time we attend to another parasite idea (worry, fear, sensation of fatigue, scruples). The fatigue is then disproportionate, abnormal. We call this mental fatigue. Then we grasp ideas less deeply and forget them sooner. The distraction, or parasite idea, has an effect like that when two typewriter keys are both touched at the same time. The machine resists and the writing is confused. So our brain becomes fatigued and we understand ideas but poorly, and we can have no experience of satisfaction or joy. A quarter of an hour's work is not equalized by another quarter hour's rest. A whole night is not enough to make up for the day's expenditure of energy. This is why we are exhausted from a hurried visit to a museum or after nervously rushing through the newspaper. If this type of labor is continued it leads at last to "overwork" (fatigue of the brain) and "breakdowns."

Geniuses of one sort or another—artists, inventors, heroes, saints—are usually silent, concentrated. Dissipation weakens by dispersing energies; concentration gathers them together, as it were, in a close bundle.

Imperfect concentration is often responsible, too, for visual defects, especially nearsightedness, farsightedness and astigmatism (that is, indistinct vision due to bad focusing). When the accommodation nerves of the eyeball are taxed by divided or imperfect attention, they put into a state of excessive tension the muscles which lengthen or shorten for the purpose of focusing upon the object. With time these muscles lose the elasticity which is necessary for accommodating the eye to vision.

That is the reason why many nervous people, by practising the *"Age quod agis"* ("Do what you're doing"), improve their concentration and often find that their vision also is bettered.

Causes of Defective Concentration—

1. Organic weakness
2. Tension of nerves and muscles
3. Lack of training or bad training of the attention
4. Some emotional disturbance, a fear or desire which pulls all thought into its wake. This is the most frequent cause.

Re-education of Productive Power

In addition to organic strengthening to counteract weakness, and relaxation exercises to counteract tension, re-education will be twofold. One phase will be more mechanical and technical, the other more mental. Let us take up the former first.

Everyone, even the mentally ill, can concentrate his attention for a moment of time. Beginning with this possibility and graduating the exercises, he can arrive at normal concentration.

The exercises here proposed are not the only ones nor are these particular exercises absolutely necessary. But they have as their guarantee the experience of the school of psychiatry at Lausanne. Whatever other method may help the victim to get out of himself and fix his attention on other ideas will be advantageous. This will be especially true if he finds it useful and pleasant.

External Visual Concentration.—If you make a dot and think of nothing else, you will have an instant's concentration. If you prolong it in a straight line without thinking of anything else, you will attain a concentration of some seconds. With your finger, then, trace in the air several large figures without interrupting their continuity. Follow them attentively. Make, for example, each of the figures below five times each.

A student came to me one day with the complaint of great mental wandering in his study. There was

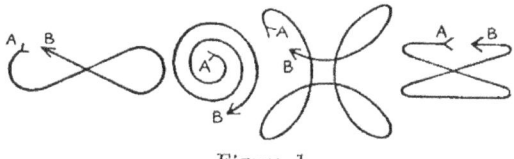

Figure 1

no particular focus-point around which his distractions would come and go. He began to do these exercises for about five minutes in the morning, again at noon, in the afternoon and at night. In four days he could do them naturally and without distractions. He then went on to do the ones illustrated below. They are a bit more difficult and demand a more prolonged attention.

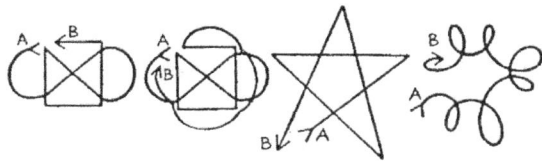

Figure 2

I also taught him to trace in the air giant capital letters and whole words in which there was no break in the continuity, always watching his finger with tranquil attention. After ten days of this somewhat artificial education he was able to leave these crutches behind and apply his attention to the book he was studying. He easily succeeded in making resumés of short paragraphs, then longer passages and even a half-page at a single reading.

A business man was on the verge of a collapse because of excessive work and the nervous tension under which he was living. He went to Dr. George W. Hall, an eminent neurologist. After the diagnosis was made that there was no acute organic lesion of any kind, he asked for a treatment which would permit him to reknit as soon as possible the rhythms of his accelerated life. Dr. Hall suggested that he have an aquarium of tropical fish built in his private office and that he spend an hour every day peacefully watching the graceful convolutions of those little creatures. The patient was a bit nonplussed but followed the prescription faithfully. Before the year was out he sent a donation to Dr. Hall's hospital as a token of gratitude for his cure. The fish were tracing out the type of manoeuvres which we here recommend.

Internal Visual Concentration.—It will sometimes be helpful to do the same manoeuvres mentally, without the aid of your hand, as if upon a blackboard. Practice this too for several days.

Auditory Concentration.—We shall explain auditory concentration in the form of an actual case. One woman found it hard to follow spoken addresses or lectures. The effort to concentrate brought on such a nervous strain that several times she had to leave the hall. And a slight noise would awaken her at night. Whether at home or in the office she could not read or write if anyone were, for instance, to move about or play a piano in her vicinity.

For several days she exercised herself in voluntarily encouraging different kinds of noises. Then she would follow the sound of a clock, saying and hearing mentally, "Tick-tock, tick-tock," for about ten times with perfect concentration. On the second day she reached fifteen and on the fourth more than twenty without a thought of anything else. To this exercise she gave at the most only five minutes each time. But she did it about eight times a day. Once she had satisfactorily obtained this auditory concentration she went on to listen voluntarily to an address or lecture. At first she listened for ten, then fifteen minutes or more without fear or distractions. When these did come her only care was to fix her attention anew on what was being said. In a month she was cured.

She also undertook to do these exercises in the midst of noise and other people's conversations. When she had no more fear of these difficulties and was no longer annoyed by the conversation of others, she could at last work peacefully and tranquilly.

Concentration in the Midst of Noise.—We recommend this same procedure to people who have to work amidst the racket of an office, or conversations or music, where the distractions are many and fatigue is so easily induced. They should practice for only a few minutes at first. Then they should do it for a longer time till they learn to be completely independent of what is going on around them. They should imitate children who can attend to their book or lesson without bothering about the shouts of their companions. It never occurs to children to make a protest against noise. In the sincere acceptance of noise is the main part of the remedy. This is also a good way to get to sleep.

Touch Concentration.—Preserve for a few seconds the sensation of hardness, cold, heat, and the like when you touch an object.

Concentration on Movement.—When walking, for example, realize now that the right foot is moving, now the left, then the whole body. For this exercise you will of course have to move slowly or you will be unable to feel these sensations.

Concentration on One Part of the Body.—Take your hand, for instance. Feel it as your own, as alive, while you hold it out before you. With a few days of practise you will after a few moments of concentration feel a slight prickling sensation in the part on which you are concentrating.

By this exercise Dr. Vittoz even cured some cases of paralysis which were of mental origin. For example, to move a paralyzed arm the patient first had to concentrate on one part of it. This would attract a greater flow of blood to that part. Then he changed the concentration and consequent flow of blood from above to below and vice versa. Finally the will could command movement again.

Concentration against Pain.—By the same method we can stop or lessen the feeling of pain from, say, an injury. By concentrating attention on the part affected by pain, *not on the pain itself or its causes,* a voluntary wave from within will neutralize the wave of pain from the injury outside. It will keep the pain, or most of it, from coming to the nerve centers and being felt.

A More Mental Form of Re-education

Lack of interest in what we read, hear or do, or the greater repulsion, attraction or importance we give to what we desire or fear, are the greatest enemies of concentration. Unreasonable fears or parasite ideas, worries or uncontrolled passions cause the most distractions. The remedy lies, as indicated above, in discovering their disturbing focus-point and then weakening and even destroying it. We shall explain this more at length in chapters IV and IX.

We must arouse interest and pleasure in what we are studying or doing by considering its utility, convenience and ease of performance. In a word we should see it in the light and warmth of an ideal (See chapter XII).

Concentration in Reading.—Fix your attention on what you are reading until you come to the first period. Rest there a few moments with conscious sensations. Read again as far as the second period and rest again, and so on until a page is completed. Repeat this exercise three times a day. This is an excellent method for re-education and is the best way to control excessive haste and anxiety to finish the reading. This haste and anxiety cause much fatigue. More concrete means for concentrating in study, in the case of healthy people as well as sick, will be found in the second part of this book under the heading "How to Think" (Chapter VII).

Neuromuscular Relaxation.—We said before that tension of the nerves and muscles (neuromuscular tension) is usually one of the causes of bad concentration, or may be produced by it. As a matter of fact, with all mental activity there is a corresponding bodily activity in nerves and muscles. Every excess or disorder in the first is accompanied by tension or fatigue in the second.

We have all observed muscular activity in external attitudes of attention. Some of these are eager movements, shortened breath, a slight bending forward of the head, stiffening of the shoulder muscles.

There are many nervous or tense people who easily tire themselves out if they read or study while seated. If instead they read or study while walking in a garden, they can keep at it much longer. This is true because there is muscular tension while they are seated. But while walking they can better relax their muscles, especially those used in breathing. There are also more frequent moments of receptivity or rest.

Another effect of hypertension is a certain tendency to overactivity when we try to surpass ourselves in vivacity and effort. We then underestimate fatigue until prostration comes.

Practice.—If you notice this tension in yourself, use the following relaxing technique. Loosen well the muscles of your forehead (without wrinkling or knitting it). Then relax the muscles around your eyes (keep a tranquil gaze like that of a contemplative). Relax and loosen your mouth (tongue, jaws and lips). Then relax the muscles of hands and feet (let them be quiet and limp and, as it were, feel the weight of gravity). Especially relax the muscles of waist and diaphragm (let your breathing be natural, deep and rhythmical).

There is a residual tension which ordinarily remains in hypertense muscles even after the rest and relaxation of sleep. The best way to eliminate this is by rhythmic exercises of the arms and legs, bending and revolving the trunk, and exercises which make the joints more flexible.

You must, however, keep in mind that this technique will have less effect if the mental causes of tension remain within us. These mental causes are insecurity with resulting fears or worries, feelings of irresistible impulse, and an excessive spirit of competition. These cause exaggerated effort and haste and are rooted in an overestimation of oneself. As a counterbalance to such tendencies, in addition to what we shall say in the chapters on Feelings (Chapters IV and IX), we here point out the tonic and calming effects of friendship or love, a reasonable ideal and a firm religious faith together with a pure conscience.

If you have nothing to lean upon before facing

the problems which each day brings, if you cannot find within yourself the equivalent of this support, you will be disturbed and tense. For the child an external support will be his mother's love. For a wife it will be her husband. For a youth it may be a faithful friend or self-sacrificing teacher or his spiritual director. And for the fervent believer it will be the help of God. One's own interior support or personal security will be strengthened by lending security or support to other people. Oftentimes widows triumph in life and spread security and joy as long as their children are small, yet feel sad, insecure and troubled when they grow up. Give to others love, help and protection and you will increase your own security, joy and peace.

Excessive effort and haste disappear when we purge our ideal of strange rivalries or stratagems and accommodate it to our strength and possibilities (see Chapter XII). But even when you succeed in life and see your human ideal attained, there will still remain in the depths of your being a fountain of restlessness and tension. You can only remove this if, when you think about the future, you find in firm, religious faith and a pure conscience an answer which will give you peace.

A Fundamental Axiom

We said at the beginning that we cannot at the same time be both fully receptive and productive. We cannot have a clear consciousness of a sensation and at the same instant be thinking of something else. By our very thinking of this other thing we cease to have that clear consciousness. And vice versa, in following out an idea and concentrating our attention on it, we cease to give clear attention to our sensations. In short, when the field of consciousness is wholly occupied by sensation there is no room for other concentration, and vice versa.

One consoling conclusion is the possibility of resting and temporarily overcoming worries, sadness, phobias and passions. On the one hand only productive power can cause fatigue. On the other hand only receptive power can bring peace and rest. We cannot at the same time be wholly receptive and productive. But with a little training we can make ourselves merely receptive even under the influence of worries and phobias. So there follows the clear possibility of acquiring this repose and mental control by means of receptivity.

A priest once confided to me that with this means alone he succeeded in dominating an instinctive fear which he had had since childhood. "I was afraid," he told me, "of cemeteries at night. So I went to one after dark. I kept my attention continually on pious thoughts or conscious sensations. Thus I succeeded in not having the feeling of fear master me even for a minute, although several times it fought hard for entrance.

"In the same way I conquered impatience in treating with a very disagreeable person. Each time his irritating words and actions provoked me to anger, I turned my attention away from them. I concentrated on observing his mental patterns, his gestures, tone of voice, or the colors of things around us. It was a kind of mental armor which kept the explosive out."

By the same simple method of having conscious sensations when an evil impulse came, a complete cure was wrought for a man tempted impulsively to wrath and suicide. A notable improvement was brought in the same way to a young man with almost unrestrainable sexual obsessions or impulses.

FROM IMPERFECT MASTERY TO CONTROL

The mentally weak or sick have no true concentration when they work or study. And during the times when they should be resting they go on thinking of their studies or business. Or they walk wrapped in worry, doubts or sadness. Even in sleep they attain no true repose. Instead they frequently pass the time in dreams. They produce much more than they receive. This may be graphically represented as in the following figure.

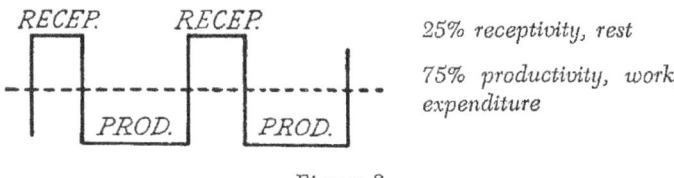

Figure 3

By concentrated work at its proper time and sensations or conscious life at other times they can avoid disorder and attain the equilibrium of persons who are mentally normal. These latter, in moments of concentration or study, think only of what they are doing. They forget everything else. At other times they either have conscious sensations or think of nothing at all. In this way the time of rest or sensation is proportioned to the time of work or concentration. Their balance of activity is pictured in the following graph.

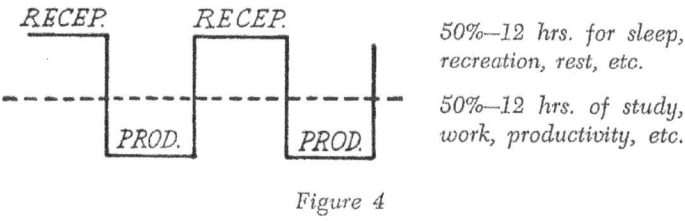

50%—12 hrs. for sleep, recreation, rest, etc.

50%—12 hrs. of study, work, productivity, etc.

Figure 4

Mental Control

We should attain such dominion over our faculties that we can pass swiftly from work to rest, from our interior world to the exterior, from concentration to sensation and vice versa, changing from graph A to B (following).

In A the shift from work to rest comes with a period of intermediate agitation, with fluctuations of work.

In B the transition from concentration to sensation is fast and immediate, without fluctuations or intermediate states.

To attain this control it will help to pass the hand of a clock mentally from one hour to another. Inter-

48] ACHIEVING PEACE OF HEART

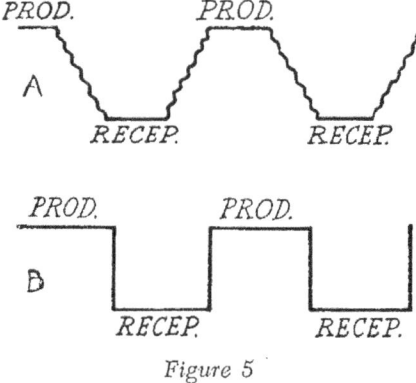

Figure 5

pose conscious sensations after concentrating on each hour for a few seconds.

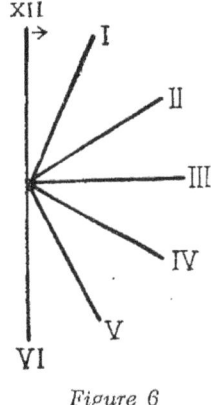

Figure 6

Do the exercise this way. Say "Twelve o'clock" and imagine the hand on twelve. Concentrate your attention there. Then rest with a few sensations. Then say "One o'clock" and mentally shift the hand from XII to I. Concentrate and rest as before. Thus cover this half of the clock in one or two minutes of intermittent concentration. Do this exercise, also, three times a day.

Use these exercises to produce a healthy habit of rest, conscious life and concentration. They directly attack mental vagueness, excess and disorder. They must be done methodically and constantly by dedicating to them several times a day a few minutes which are free from every other occupation. *Without having put them into practice you will find it hard to understand the utility of this part of the book.* Be careful in these exercises to avoid anything which is negative or depressing. Instead of reminding us of our illness or deficiency they should help us to forget it. They should convince us that we are controlling our illness by making us take more joy in the present and in the real world. They shall make us feel that we are more free and have greater mastery of ourselves. Perform them then with zest, as a sort of mental sport, without worry or anxiety, without attributing to them a greater efficacy than they have.

Maximum Normal Concentration Period

Fixed and clear concentration on a single sensation or idea, without repeating the impulse to pay attention to it, will only last a few seconds, scarcely half a minute. Yet you can pay attention to successive sensations or reasoning processes for a longer time. All in all our maximum effort at concentration will normally last about twenty minutes. We do not exceed this without placing an unnecessary strain on ourselves. We must then rest for an instant and relax our attention. This is what we do instinctively when turning the page of a book or changing our position.

This is why we should interrupt our reading after fifteen or twenty minutes and take a few moments of rest by conscious sensations. Hence also the pedagogical necessity in lectures or sermons, especially if we are talking to children, of relaxing the audience's attention with a digression, story or joke. If we do not grant the audience this rest they will take it for themselves and thus lose the thread of our discourse. In this as in most matters difficulties should be reasons for greater courage and energy, not excuses for sloth or cowardice. Just as a tree grows more luxuriantly beneath the pruning knife, so our spirit becomes stronger and more agile with the struggle.

OUTLINE DIAGRAM

Mental Activity and Re-Education

MENTAL ACTIVITY

- **RECEPTIVE**
  - What it is
    - receiving successive sensations into consciousness
    - a kind of passive attention
  - Effects
    - peace, rest, tonic, joy
  - Re-education
    - conscious sensations
    - conscious acts

- **PRODUCTIVE**
  - What it is
    - producing images, reasoning processes
    - active attention
  - Efficient
    - concentration on one idea only
    - minimal "physical" fatigue
    - maximum return
  - Defective
    - attention with distractions
    - greater fatigue
    - less return
  - Harmful
    - following several ideas at once
    - harmful effects on vision
    - causes
    - { maximum fatigue / minimum return }
  - Re-education
    - mechanical
      - visual concentration
      - concentration on sound and touch
      - concentration on one part of the body
    - mental
      - concentration in reading
      - removing worries
      - arousing interest
    - neuromuscular relaxation

- Fundamental axiom
  - you do not produce and receive simultaneously
  - so learn to rest and control yourself

- From imperfect mastery to control
  - equilibrium through
  - rapid transition
  - from concentration to sensation

- Maximum concentration period

III

Re-Education of the Will

"'I will' is a phrase rarely meant though much in use. A man who comes to realize the secret of really using his will, though today he be poor and lonely, will soon surpass all others."—Lacordaire

DEFINITION

THE WILL is a rational appetite which tends toward the good, once the good is apprehended by our intellect. It is also the executive power of our personality by which we choose and pursue definite goals and the means to those goals. Accommodated to mental treatment, the will may be described as an individual energy by which we are able freely to organize the representation of an act and freely to think about its execution. The greatest of our mental energies, if well channeled it will most quickly cure us. This energy is accumulated in deliberation and discharged in decision. It is distinct from our acts. It is free, active and guided by intelligence. Even in the case of people with nervous and emotional disturbances and conflicts, even in cases of apparent loss of will power, this energy still exists though latent and unused.

False or Ineffective Acts of the Will

Mere desire: this is passive, necessary; the presentation of a good object suffices for our will to desire it.

Vague intention, or "Having a mind to do something": this is a kind of tendency to do something; it is not even wanting it, but a vague plan or attempt to want it.

Impulse: this is being determined by external circumstances or forces; it is indeliberate, instinctive, a great force but a chaotic one.

Velleity: this is an absence of the feeling of personality; "I would like to" but not "I will."

Effective Acts of the Will

Those acts truly and fully come from our will which leave us with the persuasion and intimate conviction that they are free. Considered under their bodily aspect, we see they are only effected when we, as it were, propel them forth. We make them, so to speak, when our lungs are full of air, not when we are inhaling. A muscular contraction and speed-up of circulation accompany them. They produce a nervous discharge which is perceptible to one of experience.

This kind of act truly educates the will. It leads most quickly to a cure. Its source is will power. This is the "deliberate determination" of which St. Ignatius Loyola, Founder of the Society of Jesus, speaks in his book, *The Spiritual Exercises*. Dr. Vittoz describes this act for us by basing it upon what you could feel when placing your hand lightly on a patient's forehead.

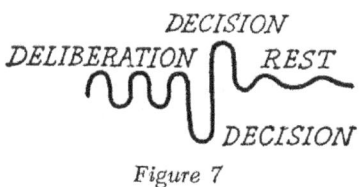

Figure 7

First you feel the pulsations, as he says, which reflect deliberation. They are similar to those of perfect concentration. Then there are one or several stronger waves which correspond to decision or discharge of the will. Finally there is the smooth rhythm of repose.

Dr. Vittoz and his students by their refined sense of touch perceived "brain pulsations" which they distinguished from the ordinary pulse. These they found useful for the external observation and control of a patient's mental acts.

Their distinction and classification, done "grosso

modo" by the Lausanne school, confirms and synthesizes what has been explained above.

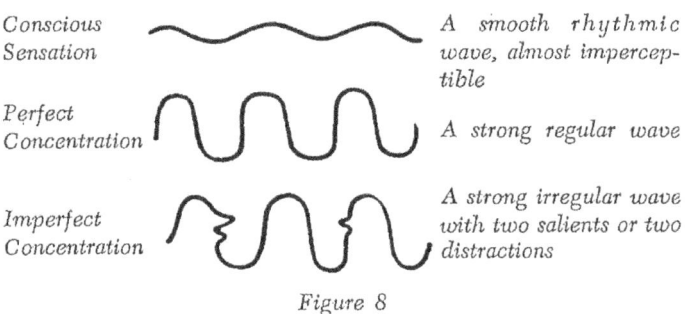

Figure 8

Note that these graphic representations of the waves give us in their general pattern the immediate impression that conscious sensations are a tonic activity of our mental system and produce rest.

Secondly, note that defective "production," or simultaneous work at several ideas, disturbs, fatigues and weakens us.

Finally, as pictured in the will curve, decision obviously produces peace and rest. Indecision, on the contrary, is a source of fatigue. For the brain then overloads itself with energies which find no outlet.

Requisites for True Acts of the Will

(1) Make the act concrete.—Picture clearly to yourself what you are going to do. Concentrate your attention on this image. The more detailed and vivid an image you form, the more force it will have. Lack of this requisite is a prime source of lack of will power in people with emotional or nervous disturb-

ances. It is hard for them to halt the flow of their ideas. Their productive power does not obey them thoroughly. They find it hard to concentrate on what they are going to do.

To concentrate well on what you plan to do, answer the following questions: "What am I going to do? When must it be done? How?" Consider also the other conditions necessary for execution. Our most noble faculty is not put in motion when it does not know where it is going. Because of this lack of precision many pretended plans do not pass from the stage of desire, or velleity or incipient intention. There is no mental discharge in them. Here we have the main cause of inefficiency in what we thought were decisions. They were too vague, not concrete.

(2) Feel the possibility of deciding.—The queen of our faculties is too conscious of its dignity to throw itself consciously into a frustration. It will not exert a force which it knows must be sterile. Once the act is made concrete, examine yourself to see whether the energy you possess is equal to the energy necessary for the act. You should feel this possibility somewhat as an athlete feels whether he has the needed muscular strength to perform some feat.

(3) Have a motive.—Our will is an energy ruled by intelligence and naturally inclined toward the good. You should perceive values, goods, motives for an act. To obtain strength of will these motives should be:

> *Objective:* good in themselves, not merely because of other considerations.
>
> *Subjective:* perceived as good for you.
>
> *Accommodated* to your individual capacity. This will be more the motive of sensible pleasure for the young, more the motive of abstract goodness for adults.
>
> *Actuated* or *recorded:* either put into action at the very moment of decision, or stored up for the moment decided upon for execution.

(4) Make a sincere will act or decision.—This is the condition most frequently absent and causing most failures of will. It consists in really determining yourself. Decision converts a plan to present or future reality. Decision makes a real actuality of what is merely possible. By decision you give the victory to a practical idea by excluding the opposite or alternatives as if impossible for you. By this sincerity you *feel* that the "Yes" or "No" is true, effective, certain. You are left with the conviction that the object of your act of will must be realized and that its existence is already assured. The deep rooted cause of our weakness and impotency is in the slackness of our willing. When something is really willed, then hitherto unsuspected energies are released even by weak organisms.

RE-EDUCATION OF THE WILL

Those who are abulic (that is, those who suffer loss of will power) because of not making true acts of the will lose the internal consciousness or feeling for them. *They should above all practice simple acts which are thoroughly willed* (for example, walking, lifting their arm, touching some object) until they recapture the internal feeling of a will act. They should then go on graduating these acts from what is more easy to the more difficult.

One young man, though educated in Catholic schools, threw over every moral restraint when he went on to the university. By habitually surrendering to impure vice he ended up in such a state of abulia and indecision that to him it seemed impossible to practice continence. He felt depressed, enslaved and annihilated in his personality. The vicious obsession was moreover obstructing his concentration in study.

It was not too hard to convince him that by re-educating his will he could remake his personality and recover his onetime vigor. In the first week of treatment he made external acts of the will eight or ten times each day by answering the following questions.

(1) *"What's up? When and how is it to be done?"* And he would make a concrete answer: "The question is whether or not to get up out of bed, walk to the right or left, and so forth."
(2) *"Is this possible for me?* If I order my feet to take me to such and such a position, will they obey me?" And he got himself to feel the feasibility of this by making affirmative replies.

When a somewhat more difficult matter would come up, he would say in a tone of absolute certainty: "Yes, I am sure I can do it!"

(3) *"Are there motives for willing this?* Yes, even if it be no more than to exercise my personality and educate myself."

(4) *"In that case shall I will it or not, Yes or No?"* And he would make the decision internally, setting aside the contrary possibility.

He experienced so much pleasure at feeling the strength of his will that on the third day he came to tell me all about it. Then he exercised himself in acts that were more difficult and required a greater conquest. Afterwards he practised acts in which his passion was involved; for example, instead of going into such and such a dangerous place, going into another. Or he would order his eyes to fix themselves on some inoffensive object instead of an exciting one. And so on.

After sixteen days he was transformed. He had won the fight. He felt himself strong, joyful and happy. He left all his bad companions. The ideal of scholarship shone anew for him. He recovered ease of concentration. And I should add that to these mental means he added the supernatural one. He also reconciled himself with God in the Sacrament of Penance.

Anyone can use this system to increase his efficiency. All he need do is exercise himself in easy external will acts. Later he should go on to more difficult acts and then to internal acts. For example, you will to think about this thing or other. When such and such an idea or fear comes to you, decide now to think of or do such and such a certain, definite thing.

The greatest enemy to will power is the *indecision* common to all such victims. There is a struggle between practical ideas. Shall they act or not? Shall they do this or what? They do not know how to grant victory to one contesting choice and put an end to all discussion by excluding other possibilities. They should be able to correct this quickly.

Remedy for Indecision

(1) When indecision comes from *lack of will power or laziness of will* you will find it helpful to practice frequent will acts even upon unimportant or indifferent matters, or those which you normally do by routine.

(2) If this indecision results from a *lack of intellectual concentration,* because you are unable to fix your attention on the act you intend to perform, then re-educate concentration. You can then easily make the act concrete and reach a decision.

(3) Sometimes indecision comes from *balanced motives for and against,* or at least it seems so. If it is an important question and you can consult a prudent person, then by all means do so. And make the decision as it seems to him. If the matter is of less importance or you are unable to consult someone, then decide quickly for either one of the two

sides. In similar circumstances some of the saints would make a short prayer and ask God to resolve the doubt by means of chance. They would then confidently accept the result.

(4) Your difficulty may come from a *variety of conflicting motives.* If other motives obscure the principal one whenever you wish to make a decision or execute it, then allow yourself to be influenced only by the motive which moved you first. For this is usually the principal one. You should make the decision at once without considering the secondary, conflicting motives.

EXECUTION

Decision introduces a great force into consciousness which carries it naturally onward toward act. If you can perform the act immediately, then this force is discharged without a new intervention of consciousness. If the execution is for some future time the order will be transmitted and reserves of energy will remain on the subconscious level. They will be ready to work automatically at the proper time unless you intervene with a counter-order or some unforeseen obstacle occurs.

For example, I decide to go visit a friend after dinner. As a matter of fact I take my hat, board the streeetcar and ride until I arrive at his house without making a new conscious act.

There are people who decide to rise at a determined time and then the subconscious which never sleeps arouses them at the exact hour. It will even do this before the hour if they are worried about it.

Once you have decided that you must accept a certain practical idea, and have excluded the opposite as impossible, never discuss it at the time of execution. This would equivalently annihilate the decision. Instead do it blindly. Suppose you decide to arise at the first sound of the alarm clock. On hearing it never stop to argue the matter. Do not stop to think whether or not you are still tired or whether it is still early. But immediately jump out of bed.

If the execution costs you some trouble or is repugnant to your instincts, in the time intervening between decision and execution do not even think about what you are going to do. For then the instinctive objections would reappear. At most think only of the good consequences which your understanding foresees.

If your decision is to avoid an action to which you are attracted by instinct, it will be better not to think of it at all. Every idea tends toward the act. If perchance you *must* think of it, then let it not be a concrete idea. An idea is more compelling the more concrete it is and the stronger impression it makes on you. Consider only the repulsive aspect of the act and its occasions, or its harmful consequences.

This is a means to perform easily acts which are subjectively heroic. Decide upon the act in the light and warmth of some principal motive. Then for the interval preceding its execution do not think about the act or the contrary motives which unconscious repugnance will present. In short, *you should not think about an act for a longer time than you need to reach a decision.* And when the moment comes, execute it blindly as if it were something automatic which it were impossible not to do.

To make the most effective use of the will, the queen of our faculties, we should accustom ourselves to follow this procedure. On feeling an impulse to do this or that, we should always leave an interval between it and carrying out the impulse. This is allowing time for deliberation. It is the same as saying, "Look before you leap." Before the act of will itself we should ask ourselves, "Shall I actually will this [something concrete]: for what motives?" In the decision itself we should answer, "I do really will it," or "It will be done." We make a firm and concrete act of the will and buttress it by feeling its possibility, usefulness and even necessity. Then we should finally clinch the matter by excluding even the thought of an opposite decision, insisting with ourselves, "It's all settled. Now we go into action."

OUTLINE DIAGRAM

Re-Education of the Will

Definition	tendency towards the good our executive power energy that is free, active, guided by intelligence			
Will acts	*false* will acts	mere desire vague intention instinctive impulse velleity ("I would like to")		
	aspects of *true* will acts	bodily: tension and circulation speed-up		
		mental	concrete object possibility felt to be so motive sincere decision	
Re-education	feel your act of will progress from external to internal acts decide the means to take			
Execution	immediate			
	long-term	do not discuss the plan decided do not even think about it till the time comes		

IV

Re-Education of the Feelings

THERE IS AN INTRICATE labyrinth of definitions and theories about feelings or emotions, their species, causes and effects. But the only point of interest in a practical manual is to know their influence on mental fatigue and weakness, and to point out some norms for channeling and governing them.

Merely speculative images, experiences and ideas pass without further ado into the archives of our memory. But there are others which are connected with feelings of fear or hope, joy or sadness, anger or love. If the feelings connected with ideas are very intense, they disturb other ideas and tend to drive them out. They attract all attention to themselves and produce commotions and alterations in the organism. Some of these alterations are a pallor or flush, shortened breath, visceral movements, secretions. At other times feelings remain hidden but active in the subconscious. Thence they disturb the workings of our mind or will.

An emotion is an emergency state in which the whole organism is prepared for action when an enemy appears, or a danger, or even a sudden stroke of good fortune. Its process may be outlined somewhat as in the diagram [1] on the following page.

THE PSYCHO-PHYSIOLOGICAL TRAJECTORY OF AN EMOTION

A. Spontaneous Phase. Let us suppose that an enemy appears before me, or a danger, or I am insulted or threatened, or that I have a vivid recollection of an injury or insult. These exciting factors come to the cerebral cortex through the senses or the imagination. If I see in them a danger to my life or a great inconvenience, a concrete judgment is immediately formed, "Danger!" or "Enemy!" And immediately the alarm is given to the hypothalamus in the center of the brain which is the engine room of the emotions. The hypothalamus stimulates the autonomic nervous system and through this and through the secretion of sympathin (an adrenalin-like compound) prepares the organism for defense or attack. The muscles become tense, heart and lungs are agitated, the glands are activated, and so on.

If the exciting factor is not very strong or lasting,

---

[1] The two phases here outlined will not necessarily be perceived as separate realities in the concrete.

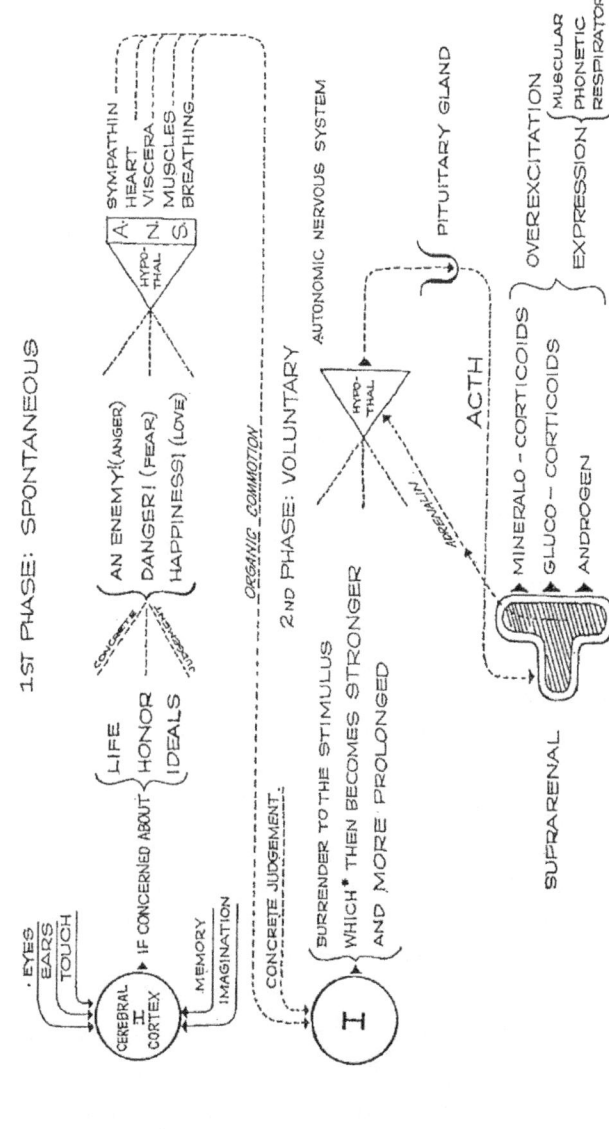

or if I do not conceive the situation to be a serious one, the commotion will soon cease of itself without causing a greater disturbance. All this would be the spontaneous or involuntary phase of an emotion.

B. Voluntary Phase. But if the exciting factor is very strong or if, when the disturbance comes to my attention, I go on thinking about it or mulling over its gravity, other effects will come about. The hypothalamus will be excited anew upon my clearer perception of the enemy or the danger or the seriousness of the situation. Not only will it get the autonomic nervous system ready for defense or attack. It will also stimulate the anterior lobe of the pituitary gland to liberate the hormone ACTH, and by means of this will overexcite the suprarenal cortex. This in turn will liberate three other groups of hormones, those which influence mineral and glucose metabolism and an androgen-like hormone. These hormones, with an action that is slower but more maintained than that of the nervous system itself, arouse the different organs to increased activity. Moreover, the adrenalin which is secreted by the suprarenal glands continues to stimulate the hypothalamus even more and so continues the expenditure of energy unless we stop attending to the exciting factor.

Hence we see that: (1) Strong and lasting emotions which are not controlled are very often causative of somatic disorders such as hypertension, indigestion, intestinal ulcers, bronchial asthma, arthritis, tachycardia, migraine, and so on.

(2) To control these emotions we must either avoid the excitant or change our method of dealing with it, and so come to modify the concrete judgment which starts or accelerates the machinery of emotion. (In Part II we shall explain this in more detail when treating of anger.)

It is also a fact that the same ideas or incidents make a great impression upon some individuals and little or none upon others. Even in the same person they make a great, small or no impression depending upon his mental or bodily condition or upon whether they take him by surprise or are foreseen. They leave little trace in persons whose backgrounds of ideas, convictions or feelings permit them to see in such happenings other features to oppose the sadness or fear, desire or worry, usually connected with the happenings. Suppose two individuals, one a miser and the other poor in spirit and loving poverty, each suffer the same loss of fortune. The first will be greatly depressed and, unless he knows how to distract himself or occupy his attention with other ideas, his sadness will eventually master him and make him lose control. The other man, on the contrary, will take his loss without shock because the background of his ideas or feelings on the subject of poverty help him to meet the misfortune undisturbed. Once the first instinctive reaction is passed, it may finally be even pleasing to him.

These ideas with a pleasant or unpleasant feeling attached have three main tendencies.

First, they tend to imbed themselves deeply, and

reappear as often as a common English word. When we fear or desire something very much, that thing attacks us at every instant. It tries to occupy our consciousness anew. It besieges and blockades us (*obsidere* in Latin). In other words we have an obsession. If it conquers us and we give it entrance it will eventually have even organic effects.

One lady, sick with the grippe, was examined by the doctor. "Have you ever had any heart trouble? It's beating very fast." The question made a strong impression on her. Once cured of the grippe she kept feeling palpitations and pains which she had never had before. Several cardiologists treated her without result. At last she consulted Dr. Vittoz who discovered her emotional fixation and with it symptoms that she had but little mental control. In a few weeks he re-educated and cured her without medicine.

Secondly, such ideas tend to become modified, exaggerated and more extensive. For example, a young man twenty-five years old, who blushed in the presence of any person at all, consulted a priest about his problem. Inquiring about his background, the priest discovered that the young man had been suffering from this affliction since he was eleven years old. One day he had been mischievous on his way to school. In school the teacher called on him for the lesson and he blushed. Asked why, he lied. This bothered him so much that next day he blushed again when asked for the lesson. Then the same thing happened while talking to his father, and later

RE-EDUCATION OF THE FEELINGS [73

on with other persons also. The priest discovered this cause and made him reproduce in imagination the circumstances which impressed him most. He made the young man repeat after him in a masterful tone, "I am before my father . . . and I am perfectly sure of myself." And he was cured.

Finally, such ideas tend to transfer themselves to other situations. Many experiments have proved this since the days of Pavlov's dog. Pleasure or displeasure, fear or embarrassment, first owe their origin to one cause, then are unconsciously transferred to some of the accompanying circumstances (conditioned reflexes).

A religious used to read at table in his community dining room. One day he was late and had to run. He got there almost out of breath. For the first few minutes his reading was punctuated with gasps for breath. He was embarrassed and blushed. On the following day in a state of absolute calm he took up the book and began to feel the same difficulty in breathing. The strong preceding impression had stayed in his subconsciousness like a well-worn idea. When similar circumstances again arose, it brought on the same organic effects which sudden fatigue produced before. The remedy lay in deliberately suggesting normal breathing and concentration on the opposite feeling. He imagined similar circumstances in which he did control himself until the contrary effect was imbedded in his subconsciousness.

THE EMOTIONAL ROOT OF NON-CONTROL

In treating of harmful mental production we indicated that the intellectual origin of mental fatigue was working with parasite ideas, with haste or fears. If we analyze the root of nervous haste in reading or study we shall find that it lies in an overvaluation of *time* and an underestimation or depreciation of *what we are doing* with our time. If we seek the cause of these fears, obsessions or phobias, we find it in a fixation, exaggeration or transference of intensely pleasant or unpleasant feelings. We do not live in the real world. We give things a greater importance than they should have because we are moved not by reason but by feelings. Our emotional center of gravity is disturbed.

Our mental world is like the planetary system. All our mental life (all our sensations, impressions, ideas, reasoning processes, deliberate will acts) should gravitate to and revolve about our will, the queen of our faculties. Just as order and equilibrium reign in the planetary system when the sun exerts its influence on the planets, so our mental life should obey our will. But if within the orbit of solar attraction a planet intruded which, instead of submitting to the sun, itself acted as a sun and exerted its own attraction upon the other plants, disequilibrium and disorder would result. This would be all the greater in so far as that new intruder sun were more independent of our sun and as its attractive force were more intense.

In the same way our mental life may be thrown off balance. The result will be a phobia, an irrational fear which we do not know how to control, a scruple or worry which pursues us incessantly, a desire, attraction or irrational impulse. The reason will be that independently of our will some troublesome feeling has remained, perhaps even on the level of consciousness. Or it may be that some mental event, previously conscious but now perhaps out of our control, continues to be active (or troublesome) beneath the level of consciousness. This intruder sun attracts thoughts, feelings and acts to its own orbit. The longer this intruder sun remains, the more satellites it will have, and the weaker and more disturbed will be our will's field of action. This disturbance, this intruder sun which finally influences even our organic functions, must ordinarily be sought among our feelings.

An examination in Massachusetts General Hospital of persons afflicted with gastric colitis had the following result: 96% were cherishing feelings of resentment; 75% lived a dejected life; 68% were tortured by remorse. The bitter wave of hatred or sorrow was spilling over into their intestines.

The Chicago Institute of Psychoanalysis discovered that many cases of asthma were a reaction against certain emotions.

One half the diabetic and cardiopathic cases examined were found to have an emotional interference as their cause or accompaniment. Many cases of arterial hypertension were improved by improving the mind.

The special composition of the blood which nourished the different organs evidently has great influence on them. We know, for instance, that by some mental process fear excites the suprarenal glands which secrete adrenalin. Even the smallest quantity of this substance modifies the blood, accelerates respiration, and rouses the organs of defense. We can imagine the result if the fear is a great and lasting one. We can come to similar conclusions regarding other emotions.

WE CAN CONTROL OUR FEELINGS

The effect of ideas with an overtone of feeling is certainly dependent on our organism. Thus children, women, the elderly and weak are more impressionable than men in robust health. But of course the idea itself has great influence on us. **Hence if we control the idea in its (1) content, (2) intensity and (3) duration, and avoid exaggeration and transference, we shall avoid those harmful effects.**

Know and Modify the Idea Itself

Dr. Vittoz used to say that we make a subconscious idea that was disturbing a patient normal again by making it conscious. Modern psychiatrists hold as probable that the harmful effects of anxiety are lessened in proportion as the cause which produces it is made more conscious. This is why many emotional conflicts are cured merely by manifesting them and making a minute examination of them. There are people who are afraid when there is no reason for fear. And when there is reason for fear, then their fear is a hundred percent greater than it should be.

An examination, even by putting them in writing, of the content of your feelings and their causes will help to diminish them. The account of conscience as practised by spiritual people has the same beneficial effect. The mere discovery that fears have been transferred from one object to another just because they chanced to be associated is usually enough to weaken or annihilate them. And as for a vague fear, merely reducing it to what is precise and concrete frequently conquers or weakens it.

Know and Destroy Transference

Very many phobias can be reduced to a conditioned reflex or an unconscious association of a certain feeling with a certain idea.

For example, every time that one man heard an explosion or the tolling of a bell an overtone of fear of death or disgrace would make him sad and worried. The feeling of fear had been associated with these sounds. He could be quickly cured if, while tranquil, he were to associate with them a memory or feeling of joy (e.g., such as comes with bells in a religious celebration), or even if he were merely to discover the basic cause of this seemingly groundless association.

Whenever another man was in a theater or church he would feel asphyxiated or at least find it hard to breathe. To avoid this he had to sit near a door. A feeling of insecurity had been associated with the idea of being shut in. He felt much better once he was made to see the connection to which he had never before adverted. He remembered that the first feeling of asphyxiation he experienced was when he awoke during a serious illness to find himself closed up in a dark room.

Whenever another victim would go even fifteen blocks from his house he would begin to feel ill and grow pale. His heart would beat as if he were about to die from a heart attack. If the distance was a short one, he was quite undisturbed. A feeling of fear had been associated with separation from his own people.

Once this type of artificial connection is known and made concrete it becomes easy to convince the patient (or ourselves) that the resulting phobias are artificial and absurd. Sometimes this alone is enough for a cure. In these cases we must manage to rouse a conscious association of an opposite or at least different feeling with the disturbing idea. If we can do this while we are tranquil or far removed from the incitement, we shall find it relatively easy. This consciously induced connection will afterwards be unconsciously reproduced when we are again in contact with the occasion. The former unpleasant association will be destroyed and the phobia cured.

For example, a certain young man who was unable to swallow pills was made to reproduce the situation in which the unpleasant feeling so disturbed him. He imagined vividly that he was putting one in his mouth and then associated the opposite feeling with this imaginary action. That is, he consciously attended to the feeling of not fearing, of serenity, naturalness. With the feeling in his *tone of voice* he would say, "I have the pill in my mouth . . . and I am unruffled by it . . . I *can* swallow it and . . . I shall swallow it without difficulty." While he was repeating this for the second time with a true tone of security in his voice I noticed disappear from his face a certain contraction which fear had produced. I brought him a glass of water. He took the pill and swallowed it easily.

Sometimes you will have to go deeper into this feeling (which the patient recognizes as absurd) and discover the forgotten tendency which made it once seem reasonable. When this had been discovered by psychic exploration (e.g., by tests) and eliminated or shifted to a more worthy object, you will have solved the puzzle.

Diminish the Idea's Intensity

The intensity of an idea depends on three factors.

(1) *Its quality.*—The more concretely an idea is represented, the more motive force it has. The more spiritual or abstract it is, the less motive force. That is why orators speak to the imagination to obtain an immediate result, a feeling. But when they want a lasting effect they try to convince the understanding.

(2) *Its quantity.*—The force of an idea is greater in proportion to its closer association with other ideas, experiences or feelings, and to the degree to which they are more striking.

(3) *Its duration.*—A passing emotion, fear or sadness leaves little trace in the organism or mental background. But if it remains too long it can modify them to a notable extent. It can attract into its orbit (as we said of the intruder sun) more and more thoughts and acts, and cause lasting disorder.

In several parts of South America I witnessed the following custom, a very pious one, if you will, but not very Christian. And it is by no means in accordance with mental hygiene. Women there will remain in mourning for months and months without going out of the house or admitting any distractions. When the period of mourning is over many of them have become nervous cases. Because it persisted, the depressing atmosphere of mourning destroyed their control.

Take the idea then that is bothering you and strip it of its sensible counterpart, its importance and concrete details. Break the links it has with other phenomena of your experience. Do not consciously dwell on it but, as mentioned heretofore, substitute for it a contrary thought and feeling, or at least a different one. In making this substitution search for other ideas which appeal to the senses as much as possible. Symbols will have a strong appeal to your (or the patient's) imagination. Associate these ideas with important living realities. Repeatedly pass them through your mental field of consciousness that, like a snow-ball, they may gather round them as large a number of mental elements as possible.

EXAGGERATED IMPRESSIONABILITY

If something makes too much of an impression on us we can be sure that we give it a greater importance than it has. This will depend on our bodily weakness, previous education, or lack of rational reaction against the feeling or instinct. But if we go to the very bottom of an emotional disturbance we shall find in it a *departure from reality*. This can happen in three ways.

We may be giving it a *false interpretation* (as in the case on p. 60, regarding the sound of bells or explosions). A scrupulous person does this when he sees moral responsibility where there is none.

Perhaps we are not *accepting the reality* which is imposed on us (for instance, a disgrace or some limitation). There will then be restlessness, uneasiness, sadness.

We may be *building up an absurd reality* for ourselves. An apparently good idea may be really harmful. Or we may be aspiring to what is above our strength. There will be tension because of the disproportion between desires and their possibility of fulfillment. Or there will be a conflict of feelings because our scale of values is upset. We think that a good is being offered but find ourselves with the evil which necessarily comes with it. The hierarchy of values is at stake. It is thrown into confusion by instincts or our lower mental activities. These do not perceive higher realities.

The Root of Exaggerated Impressionability

We must seek for this on the level of our lower mental activities. These do not perceive higher realities and take us away from the true reality of things, of life and of our own personality. Exaggerated impressionability is rooted in the following instincts: those of self-preservation, domination and reproduction. There is an innate *tendency to preserve* our physical, bodily nature by the reaction of flight from danger and bodily death without bothering about what is spiritual and eternal. There is also a *tendency to win out over others* and increase our own earthly goods or reputation without taking into account whether this impedes other, still greater goods. There is, finally, a *tendency to seek pleasure for one part* of our being even if it be to the detriment of the whole. This is also an impulse to flee from pain and hardship although these may bring higher goods to us. The right to our inheritance is sold for a mess of pottage. Sexual or alcoholic pleasure is sought even though ruinous to health.

We do not take into account the true reality of man. Man is not only body but spirit also. He is not only earthly and temporal but heavenly and eternal. We do not even take our own personality into account. For we refuse to accept limitations imposed on us by heredity or environment. As a result, the emotional center of gravity is thrown off balance.

This center of gravity in man is the sublime goal given him by the Creator. Man is to dispose of himself according to the good pleasure of the Infinite Being so that afterwards he may enjoy Him for all eternity. Whoever realizes the sublime dignity of being able to fulfill at each moment the ideal God sets for us, that is, "to want what He does and do what He wants," and realizes that this cannot be impeded by sickness or poverty or another's evil or injustice, such a person will never suffer a lasting mental disturbance. The saints understood this sublime goal and lived it and they are, thus, models of self-control. For this reason, too, believers who suffer emotional disturbances will do very well to add to scientific methods the still more effective method of the *Spiritual Exercises* [1] of St. Ignatius Loyola. By meditating on this great truth in his first exercise, called the *Principle and Foundation*,[2] they will bal-

---

[1] A practical manual which outlines considerations and meditations to lead to the reformation and sanctification of one's personal life. These spiritual exercises, continued through several days, are commonly known as a "retreat," or "making a retreat."

[2] According to St. Ignatius the *Principle and Foundation* of our whole spiritual life reads as follows:

"Man was created to praise, reverence and serve God, Our Lord, and by this means save his soul. All other things on the face of the earth were created for man, to help him pursue the end for which he was created. Hence it follows that he should use them insofar as they help him toward his end, and should abstain from them insofar as they obstruct him. So as far as it is permitted our free will to do so and is not forbidden, we should make ourselves indifferent to all created things, in this sense that for our part we do not seek for health rather than sickness, riches rather

ance their center of gravity again and will feel their fears and worries disappear in the deepest peace of soul.

In Lima where I received a great deal of real help in missionary propaganda from an active and businesslike lady, I stood in admiration of the serenity which the following thought habitually brought her in spite of contradictions and failures. "In comparison with God, the Infinite Being, all men are like a little grain of sand. And how much less am I? But if this atom can bring a smile to the Infinite Being, why be lost in worry about whether other atoms are praising Him or not? And why lose time thinking merely about myself, my illnesses, virtues or defects?"

Preventive Remedy

Begin at the root cause first. Fix the hierarchy of values firmly in the understanding by a good moral and religious education. Form a correct appreciation of what is lasting and eternal as superior to what is but temporal and passing. Set the total good of your whole being above the partial good of your body alone. Illuminate and direct your instincts toward their right road and goal. Elevate them by knowledge and faith to heights with which they are themselves unacquainted.

---

than poverty, honor rather than disgrace, a long life rather than a short one, and similarly in all other matters. We should desire and choose only what better leads us to the end for which we have been created." (*Exercitia Spiritualia*, in *Thesaurus Spiritualis Societatis Iesu*, Bruges, Desclée, 1932, pp. 34-37.)

You must strive to appreciate and work toward your total good. You must have a self-love which is not creeping, earthly or material but higher, spiritual and eternal. It must be a love of the life and glory which will not end, a love of suffering dignified by the ideal of bearing it as God's will, a disinterested love of others. If you have supernatural Faith and Charity, love your neighbor because in him you see your Creator disguised in his defects. Thus you can love and serve God with greater merit.

You can attain this by meditation on higher goods and practice of the virtues. The more you strengthen your higher mental activities by the understanding of higher values and by positive decisions for good, the more you will be immune from the disorders of lower instincts. In the case of the saints this dominion of reason and right morals reaches its culmination. Disgrace, humiliation and temporal dangers caused them no worries whatsoever.

Secondly, in your conduct avoid any ideas or surroundings, sights or acts which favor distorted tendencies. Block unlawful satisfaction of instinct for this engraves and stamps false values into your very being.

Direct Cures for Exaggerated Feelings

1. Discover the origin of the evil through the laws of association, testing study of dreams, and the like. Look for exaggeration or transfer of feeling, the mental fact which is the root of a worry. Then take it apart and destroy it by means of conviction, suggestion and re-education. Strengthen yourself by implanting the opposite feeling deep in the subconscious. Sometimes it will be enough to recall when and in what circumstances you first felt similar symptoms.

2. *Discover the forgotten and now subconscious reasoning process.* Every irrational feeling will seem a logical conclusion of a more or less subconscious reasoning process which is invalid or exaggerated, and is now in part forgotten. To annihilate or straighten out sentimental abnormality it is enough to make these steps which are now erased in the sands of time stand out clearly once again in consciousness. See logically and exactly the irrational or exaggerated part in the reasoning process.

3. *Implant the contrary feeling.* At the same time two opposed feelings cannot dwell in one and the same subject. If excessive repression, instilled fears or unconquered dangers have formed within you an unconscious source of insecurity and a great tendency to fear, there will be an apt feeding ground for phobias, doubts and scruples. Replace this with an equal or greater overtone of value, security or boldness and you will return to normality.

How can this be done? The will can do this in one jump if it feels the *possibility* of the act; for example, "In such and such a circumstance I shall be secure, I shall keep control." But since feelings are usually hard to manage there are few people who experience a feeling that the act is possible. Enter then by another route. Go from the exterior to the interior. Make use of the body's influence on the soul. It is certain that "whoever sings kills his pains." But even the timid soul who clenches his fists, fixes his glance and says with conviction, "Forward!" feels his own worth being reborn. When a pious man finds himself lukewarm and dry (with no feeling of devotion), yet takes a devout posture and prays with the *tone* of humility and confidence, he soon comes to the *feeling* of devotion. If the soul influences the body, the body also truly modifies the mental activity of the soul.

Live out then in your imagination the circumstances which in real life dismay you. During this imaginary experience describe with a tone of conviction the emotional state in which you should be, the one which would please you or is that of normal people. If this tone of security is very intense it will finally produce a proportionate feeling and, as in the case of uncontrolled blushing on p. 55, you will be freed of the phobia.

Fr. Laburu tells of the case of a young man from the country whom a common locust would throw into a panic. If he saw one nearby he would begin to tremble, move away and break into full flight. This was unavoidable and he would almost throw himself out of the window if he could find no other means of exit. Fr. Laburu had him imagine that a locust was flying through the door and then say to himself, imitating the tone of security with which

the priest spoke, "And I am just as calm as before."
"The locust is coming near," the psychologist would
say, and the patient would repeat this and imagine
it vividly. He would start to shift his position but on
repeating, "I am still calm; it makes no difference to
me," he would really grow calm. Again the priest
would say, "The locust is right next to me. It is in
my hands" (He had had one brought in a small
bottle) ... "It is in my hands" (He had him take the
bottle) . . . "And my appearance is unchanged."
Hardly had he repeated this last phrase in a tone of
great control when a deep breath and an open smile
made known his complete liberation.

4. Form within your mind a system of ideas, sensations, actions and desires, a framework which is a favorable background to the feeling you wish to retain. This feeling will annihilate the contrary feeling. Its very presence will help you to avoid a clash or struggle and resultant exaggeration in your emotions. Thus a timid person should think, speak and work with courage and boldness, or *as if* he had these qualities.

5. *By meditation* on the higher goods of your whole being or on eternal goods, weaken the force of instinct. Weaken also the attraction of what satisfies one particular organ of your being, or brings passing, temporary satisfaction to mere instinct.

6. *Work as if* you had the true or noble feeling you desire, or *as if* you did *not* feel the contrary tendency

or repugnance. Such acts will produce the noble feelings.

7. *By elimination exercises* habituate yourself to the practice of introducing this intruder sun (phobia, obsession) voluntarily into your consciousness, and immediately banishing it. To become skilled in this practice act as follows.

(a) Choose three or four objects and place them on a piece of white paper. Take one of these in your hand and put it aside. Then close your eyes and see that the object separated stays eliminated from your mind. In the same way, with your hand and mind both, remove the remaining objects until none of them is left in consciousness.

(b) Write three or four numerals mentally and then mentally erase them.

(c) Repeat the same exercise with three or four letters or words.

(d) Finally, when enough control has been obtained, sum up the cause of your weakness in a word or phrase, write it upon your mind and rub it out. Note that when you voluntarily implant the phobia or obsessing idea and it is not imposed by the subconscious, the usual disturbance is not provoked. Through such mastery these ideas will gradually disappear from your mental background, at first temporarily but at last for good and all.

8. *Concentrate on the opposite—*

(a) *Concentrate on the image or feeling of calm and peace.* Find in your past, or decide upon now, a feeling or memory of moral and physical tranquillity, for instance, a landscape, melody, prayer. Concentrate as much as you can on this sensation until you again relive it.

(b) *Concentrate on the image or feeling of energy and strength.* Try to feel anew your own moral force. Remember energetic moments of your life. The orator will find these in a discourse, the merchant in a successful business affair, the soldier in a battle, and so forth. Reproduce these moments mentally. If you have never really had this experience, strengthen yourself by understanding what energy means. Use images or comparisons which are accommodated to your own mental make-up and which penetrate more deeply into the subconscious. With a little perseverance you can attain this feeling of strength.

(c) *Concentrate on the image or feeling of control.* This is a consequence of the preceding. If anyone can be tranquil or energetic when he wishes then he evidently has control. Try to verify this control in yourself at the present moment and continue until you develop and implant the exact feeling of this faculty. Do these concentration exercises for a few moments at first, then for a longer time. Repeat them several times a day in different or difficult circumstances until they penetrate into the unconscious. A feeling of control with an origin like this cuts out the root of phobias.

INDIRECT CURE FOR EXAGGERATED FEELINGS

When the origin of trouble remains unknown or difficult to banish, the indirect method of cure is called for. This will be to remove satellites from the intruder sun. Do not voluntarily allow satellite feelings or acts aroused by them to remain in your consciousness. Sweep them out immediately and occupy your attention with other acts, sensations or concentrations which are voluntarily and fully conscious.

Reinforce the unity of your "mental solar system" with new thoughts and conscious and voluntary acts. It would be hard for ideas and feelings thus to become deformed. And those already deformed will return to normal. For consciousness focuses our thoughts and automatically makes them more clear and normal. And the fact that they are voluntary does away with their chaotic and disturbing force.

SCRUPLES

After a lecture a lady came to see me who had been suffering for seventeen years from persistent scruples. These had stolen away all her peace and joy. She could not go to Communion unless Confession had immediately preceded it. Even then she went in fear and trembling. She seemed quite discouraged and in a decline. I proved to her that her illness was not moral but mental. I managed to convince her that she had nothing to fear for her soul but that her health was in danger. I explained that the working of a scruple was not intellectual but emotional. For example, there were one or more ideas which caused fear within her and established this feeling in the unconscious. From this unconscious level they bothered her by arousing fear of sin, either by an association of similar images or, when she felt depressed, similar feelings.

I explained to her the conditions for mortal sin: full consciousness and a deliberate act of the will in a serious matter. These conditions were of course not verified in her case. By thus eliminating the root of fear she could promise herself that in the future she would not fear the scruple but discredit it. She would substitute a conscious sensation for it whenever it arose. By means of conscious acts, each time repeated more frequently, she began to come out of her merely subjective world and live in the objective order. She was cured by the time she had come for two interviews. When I saw her again six months later she was healthy, joyful and happy. The scruples only returned once, during a mental crisis occasioned by the death of her father. But she mastered them in a very short time.

Method for Handling Scruples

What should a scrupulous person do in the concrete? First, he should be convinced that his illness is mental rather than moral. What should we say to someone who comes up to a priest and keeps saying, "Father, save me. I have such a toothache I know

I'm going to hell." The answer should be, "Go see your dentist, but don't think that you are lost because of a reason like that." The scrupulous person must be told something similar. "Persistent scruples indicate that you have some psycho-somatic illness. Look over the mental symptoms which are listed on p. 12. Then make use of the remedies which are described in this book. But don't you worry about your eternal salvation."

1. He should increase his conscious life and live in the present. The "Age quod agis" ("Do what you're doing") is almost nullified in a scrupulous person.

2. He should re-educate his powers of concentration by forming the habit of thinking of only one thing at a time. The scrupulous man does not know how to separate himself from his obsession when he is studying, conversing or working.

3. He should above all strengthen his will by means of repeated decisions. These latter are almost extinguished in him.

4. He should exact of himself blind obedience to his director, an obedience which is founded upon supernatural faith. He should recognize that he is blind, that he needs a guide, and that for the time being he has a right not to be guided by or make changes in accordance with what his disturbed conscience tells him. He should follow what his director says to do. And in moments of doubt he must adhere to what has been determined or resolved upon at a more tranquil time or with the director's aid.

Once upon a time there was a blind man, led along by his guide, who all of a sudden stopped and said, "I can't go another step; I *see* a deep pit in front of me." The guide answered, "You do not see what is really there but something in your imagination. Let's go ahead. You leave the worrying to me." So it is with the scrupulous person.

5. He should not be moved by doubts or a "perhaps," but only by evidence.

6. He should be content with human security about salvation or the state of grace. He should not desire to have the kind of security or certitude proper to God's knowledge or that of men who are in heaven (the kind that excludes all possibility of the opposite). Thus he will help to bring about that state of confidence which is so pleasing to God.

7. He should increase this confidence by repeated concrete acts, even if the effort to overcome the contrary feeling calls for heroism on his part.

8. He should fight against the unconscious feeling of fear or doubt which is the remote root of scruples. He should frequently repeat thoughts, sentences and acts of courage and confidence.

For practical instructions on how to re-educate feelings consult chapter nine in the second part of this book. All these procedures are mental *coups d'état*. These are resolutions and assaults against diseased and cowardly ideas which tend to monopolize your conduct. Resolve to set this revolution afoot and you will be done with the indecision, inactivity and mediocrity which blunt your faculties.

Once St. Bernard was so beset by scruples that, almost in despair, he went into a church and said to Our Lord, "If I am going to curse You throughout all eternity in Hell, at least I want to love and praise You in this life." And he gave free rein to sentiments of love and praise of God. He walked out of that church cured. This strong feeling and positive emotion of love had destroyed the negative emotion of fear which had been causing so many scruples in him.

OUTLINE DIAGRAM

Re-Education of the Feelings

- Ideas
  - with an overtone of feeling
  - which make an impression on the senses
- They tend to
  - engrave themselves through sense impressions
  - exagerate themselves through passion
  - transfer through association
- They are obstructions
  - an intruder sun with its attraction
  - occupies and disturbs the field of consciousness,
  - interferes with our organs
- Re-educate by modifying the idea
  - making its content conscious
  - rectifying its exaggerations
  - destroying its false conclusions
  - moderating its
    - intensity
    - duration
    - quantity
    - quality
- Re-educate by modifying its overtone of feeling
  - its root
    - departure from reality
      - falsifying it
      - not accepting it
      - exaggerating it
    - the instincts
  - prevention
    - hierarchy of values
    - strengthen higher mental activities
    - avoid
      - bad environments
      - undue acts
  - cure
    - discover the root
    - discover the forgotten basic reasoning process
    - root out contrary feelings
    - concentrate on the opposite
    - form a favorable background of ideas
- Indirect method—remove satellite ideas
- Method for handling scruples

V

Resumé of Re-Educational Treatment

Once convinced that illness or weakness comes from disorders in your mental activities together with alterations in your nervous and muscular system, follow this health decalogue.

I. Begin by learning how to rest. Exercise naturally the easiest of mental acts, *conscious sensations*. This is at once a tonic and sedative. If tension and fatigue are very great, first take a few days rest. Change your environment or occupation, or travel.

II. Then go on to perform perfectly and without tension the second, more active mental act. Concentrate your attention on *a succession* of sensations, images or reasoning processes which you remember from the past or now elaborate in your imagination. Emphasize single-mindedness in your work.

III. In the second or third week, without wholly abandoning the previous exercises, strengthen your will by means of *decisions* that are concrete, progressively more difficult and punctually executed. Sweep out all indecision.

IV. Once your faculties are trained, correct whatever *abnormality* there may be in your feelings. To this end *first modify the idea or image* which produces them and substitute for it (as far as it appears in consciousness) sensations and concentrations which are clearly distinct and, so far as possible, also pleasant.

V. Then *modify* the emotional overtone of that idea or feeling which is bothering you. Do this first *by means of reasoning:* "This feeling of mine is irrational. Others are not bothered by it; it does not sadden them as much as it does me. I should react as others do, as a standard citizen."

VI. *Associate another, different feeling* with that idea. Bring the idea consciously to mind and then imagine other consequences and live out the other feeling which you will have prepared beforehand.

VII. *Arouse the contrary feeling* in yourself and make it penetrate even to the subconscious by imagining it vividly and speaking about it with the tone of voice peculiar to the feeling you wish. And work *as if* you already had it. Associate this strong feeling of security or courage, for instance, with the idea which formerly produced disturbance or fear. (Remember the case about the locust.)

VIII. Simultaneously with this whole treatment *repair the expenditure* of nervous and muscular energy which mental tension produces by accustoming your muscles to exercise and due relaxation. Do this both for the time of waking and sleeping. Waste no nervous energy in useless movements or tense postures.

IX. *Avoid the formation of toxins* by keeping away from foods which cannot be easily digested. Get rid of the toxins which do form by means of exercise and sweating and regular elimination. Build up your cells, nerves and muscles through healthy breathing and an adequate diet.

X. *Accept the reality* which cannot be modified. Found your ideal upon it. Fill out your human ideal with sublime truths which are eternal and divine.

APPLICATIONS AND PRACTICAL ADVICE FOR
MALADJUSTMENTS OF PERSONALITY

Know Yourself

Weakness or illness is no mere imagination or fiction. Symptoms felt in head, heart or digestive apparatus are real symptoms. In general, however, they are not caused by a lesion in your organs, but by uncontrolled mental activity or the chaotic subconscious. Specialists, when consulted, will agree about the integrity of the organs. So there should be no further worry about their decision. You must attend to and convince yourself of the fact that these symptoms owe their origin and intensity to uncontrolled thought about them and about the illness which seems to afflict them.

The practical conclusion will be not to think of the symptoms or illness voluntarily. Rather practice thinking voluntarily about the clinical decision. Feel your complete health and organic efficiency. To know the mental nature of the illness and to locate the struggle on its true ground will be fifty per cent of the cure. The other fifty per cent is in confidence and faith in the method, together with the time factor.

Think of Others

No one who lives for himself alone lives as fully or produces as much as he who lives for others and does good for others. When you are dominated by your unconscious mental activities, you lead a negative life which is colored by a sickly egoism. You are always thinking of your own troubles and finding ways to lessen them. You can find no time to busy yourself with others or do any positive and progressive work. You see the enemy everywhere and are wholly taken up with fleeing from him.

Such a person lives, as Fosdick puts it, as if in a room lined with mirrors. Wherever he looks he sees himself. But when he busies himself with others, several of these mirrors are changed into windows through which he can see other faces, other lives and other more pleasant landscapes.

You will also find great help in a noble ideal. This may be professional or religious. Let it be some unselfish dedication of your work either out of patriotism, love of your neighbor, or from some religious motive.

I knew a young doctor who was exhausted by his studies and first labors. He was crushed by insomnia, obsessions, fatigue and a sickly egoism. Then he decided to take a trip to rest and distract himself. On his arrival at a Chinese port, a missionary invited him to visit his hospital. He began to interest himself in the illnesses of those good people and lent them his professional services out of compassion. He ended up by remaining as the head of the establishment. He forgot his own ills and was completely cured.

Practice Singleness of Thought

The general cause, remote or proximate, of these mental illnesses is a kind of double thought. Or it is an occupation with several ideas at once (obsessions, fears, worries). Practice singleness of thought, then, in order not to increase your ills.

Imitate St. Bernard, the most active and busy man of his century. On his shoulders rested the responsibility for his monastery, the composition of admirable books, consultation with princes and even the business of the universal Church. When he entered a church he used to say, "Thoughts of Bernard, remain outside." And he would concentrate on his prayers in peace.

Practice Confidence

To lessen the force of an obsessing idea, a feeling of sadness or worry, you must oppose to it an intimate persuasion that everything in this world passes. Imagined ills are always greater in our minds than they are in reality. Fears of insanity, heart failure or sudden death which many nervous people have, are never realized. Experience confirms this and doctors attest to it.

Have confidence in your own health and do not be bothered by trivial symptoms of illness. Our organism is so complicated and so exposed to contrary influences that it naturally cannot function for a single day without some friction among its many parts. You may truly say, "This is nothing. It will soon pass away." Remember that however little your attention is worriedly fixed on a sensation it is thereby disquieted, increased and exaggerated. Conversely, when you shift attention to a different matter the evil lessens and gradually disappears.

Never did fear or discouragement put off the arrival of threatening evils. What fear or discouragement really does when exaggerated is to dissipate and exhaust the forces and strength you need to go out and resist those evils. If they must come, let them not, by thought, begin to torture you before the time.

Profit by Moderate Discussion

Discuss the matter freely with a prudent and experienced person. Thus you will lessen the discouragement, sadness, worry or fear, and calm the tension. Apart from discussion and consultation with specialists it is better not to speak of your illness or symptoms. The less you think of them, the less they will bother you.

This mental tryranny over you will be softened by freely talking it over with God in prayer if you accept what you have to suffer with great confidence in His love and almighty power.

Suffering is like a perfume. If you open it to human egoism the fragrance evaporates unperceived. If you open it to God it rises to Him like incense and comes down to you again like a heavenly dew. "To carry a splinter in one's heart," says Gar-Mar, "and talk of something else is the feat of a hero."

Exercise Conscious Life

When you are not engaged in intellectual work rest your mind by receiving conscious sensations with an easy, peaceful attention to the things of the external world. And when doing mental work exert yourself in concentrating all your attention there. Forget the past, future and yourself. In the beginning you will do this easily for a few moments. Then by progressive increase of attention you will attain normal concentration.

The root of the evil is in domination of conscious mental activity by the unconscious. Now the acts prescribed above are in themselves insignificant. Yet because they are fully conscious and often repeated during the day, they attack the root of the evil directly. They produce a reaction of greater joy, peace and mastery.

Don't Be Discouraged

Do not think it strange if in the morning you notice a greater sensation of the symptoms, discouragement or fatigue, and if fatigue is less and sadness almost gone by the afternoon or after doing some work. The reason is that the unconscious is in control during sleep. And there is danger after awakening of continuing under its disturbing influence. After some controlled acts, however, joy returns again and our vigor is rejuvenated.

Nor should you wonder at the periodic appearance of enthusiasm and discouragement, progress and apparent setbacks. This happens in many mental and nervous illnesses.

Fight Pessimism

An uncontrolled imagination drives a man toward pessimism and exaggeration of his troubles, and hence to discouragement and despair. For sad events and experiences, at one time conscious but now perhaps forgotten, continue to be active on the unconscious level. They tend to add a pessimistic overtone to all mental images. If we reflect on our thoughts and feelings we shall see that even insignificant beginnings can have terrifying consequences.

A brief daily examination in writing of the course of your pessimistic imaginings will quickly convince you of this. You will then belittle those fears, troubles and worries. If you discount your fears by 90 percent you will be closer to reality. Give no importance then to imagined ills or fears for the future. Better still, once you recognize the error or exaggeration of your unconscious mental associations, deliberately come to the opposite conclusion: enthusiam, joy, courage, optimism. For, as Father Gar-Mar again said, the shadow of the cross is often larger than the cross itself. So black, so sad, so crushing are the crosses we dream up for ourselves.

Keep Busy

Employ your time well and so distribute it among different tasks that by keeping yourself busy you have no time for worry. To enable the factor of feeling to intervene here let your undertakings be in the possible and practical order. Make sure they are useful and interesting. Only when the sick imagination finds the field of consciousness unoccupied will it be able to torture you with its sad and discouraging exaggerations. *Idleness and the lack of an ideal produce more neurotics than work ever does.*

A young bride, her mother told me, used to live tormented by fears. One fear was that she would lose her mind. She bore a son, and still the fears continued. In the course of time she had five more children and because she was not rich she had to do all her own housework. Hardly could a worry take shape when a child's wail would bring her flying to its side. Or two of them would start a squabble and she would be off to calm them down. Or she had to get a meal ready, or the ironing board was calling her. Or rain threatened to wet her laundry that was stretched on the line to dry. Some urgent household task would always be taking up her whole attention and coming just in time to kill worries at their first stirring.

The famous Jesuit scholar, Fr. Wassman, conquered his own depression by taking up the study of ants. In this field he later became so pre-eminent that the whole world marveled at his books.

Foster Joy and Optimism

Insist upon joy and optimism as opposed to the sadness and discouragement which sometimes seem so natural. Do this by briefly changing your occupation and busying yourself with thoughts, readings and conversations which make the mind happy and elevate it. Do not pretend to drown melancholy in alcohol for, as a modern author says, drinking does not drown our troubles but only irrigates them.

The central powerhouse which supplies current to our organs is optimism, either instinctive or acquired. Feelings of joy and health stimulate blood circulation and accelerate nutritional processes. If you doubt your forces and think yourself sick you are already beginning to be sick. Then the central powerhouse has lowered its potential. All lights grow dim. Your organs do not work so well. Sad passions, such as fear, worry, discouragement, agitation, anger, scorn, anxiety, make us realize the truth in the common phrase, "It makes me sick!"

All joy is curative and all discouragement tends to increase our troubles. Gladness is a swimming pool of health where we should bathe each day. Chapter eleven of this book (on happiness) will help you produce this effect.

Get Down To Work

If you suffer from any of these personality maladjustments remember that there is no lesion in your higher faculties, above all in your will. What happens is that you do not know how to use them. These faculties are marvelous forces. When well directed they are capable of transforming any mental pattern and curing any abnormality. But you must know how to avail yourself of their benefits. This is easily attained by re-education. You have the cure in your own hands. A little constancy and method is enough.

Your thoughts are the limit of your activities. No one takes a single step further than his convictions. If you imagine to yourself that you cannot do this or that, you will never do it. "Possunt quia posse videntur," the old Romans used to say. "They can because they think they can." Aside from the times when you need the ministrations or advice of a professional physician, your six best doctors are sun, water, air, exercise, diet and joy. They are always there waiting for you. They cure your ills and do not cost you a cent.

PART TWO

•

Applications and Methods

The kind of life many of us are forced to live in the modern world is fatiguing and hinders rest even in sleep. It makes tranquil and deep thought more difficult. It stifles the will and confuses acts of the will with mere impulses. It exalts feelings, lets the sexual instinct run riot, kills all deep satisfaction and true happiness. It deadens or annihilates ideals. The following applications and methods of re-education, personality readjustment and self-completion follow logically from the first part of this book.

VI

How to Rest

Whoever knows how to rest at the right time will double his efficiency and not waste his health.

RESTING WHILE AWAKE

In an Acute Crisis of "Overwork" or Mental Fatigue

WHEN THE FEELING of fatigue is accompanied by sad and depressing thoughts, it is intense and hard to control. The first remedy is to forget yourself and your illness. Specialists obtain this effect organically and violently by injections or electric shocks which produce forgetfulness or artificial sleep. However, in many less serious cases we need not take such extreme measures. Similar results can be obtained through less violent and more natural means; for example, a few days' travel or a change of dwelling or occupation. Enliven yourself with amusements which will arouse enthusiasm and prevent depressing memories. Avoid remaining inactive or unoccupied. Idleness is no solution. If depressing feelings find the field of consciousness unoccupied they will at once occupy it themselves and begin to torment you. In short, be objective. Act during the day as a receiver of impressions from the external world so that you give no place or time to the interior world of subjective thoughts and feelings. Later on let the work of re-education begin by means of conscious sensations and voluntary concentrations.

In Normal Fatigue

Since this comes from the working of your productive power make yourself receptive by means of conscious sensations.

Apply the sense of *sight*. Let the object penetrate within you exactly as it is, without subjective modifications. Make no comparisons. Do not reason about causes and effects. Otherwise you will still be producing ideas. Look at things just as children do, naturally, without anxiety, without wanting to embrace all the details. Contemplate, for example, a lamp, a landscape, a flower, a color, the details of some object. Get the overall effect. Absorb yourself in it. With practice this will day by day become more easy and successful.

Hear a near or distant noise. Retain consciousness of it for a few seconds. Or even notice the lack of noise. Open up the sense of hearing without forced attention. Repeat these acts five times each hour of the day. With these exercises you can calm irritation and hypersensitivity to sound.

Touch and feel the coldness or hardness of five objects. In each case notice the first impression on the sense.

Walk slowly, deliberately. An excellent relaxing exercise is that used by a student who had a bad case of overwork. He could scarcely pay attention to what he was doing for more than three quarters of an hour. He had to attend three classes a day which were interrupted by five minute recess periods. These he dedicated to scientific breathing and exercise. He would take five steps while inhaling deeply through the nose, feeling the air in the upper part of the nose near the forehead (not at the nostril openings for this closes them). Then he would exhale smoothly and passively through the mouth while taking eight or ten steps more. Meanwhile he kept his attention on hearing the air as it passed through his nose, and feeling his steps. By thus keeping himself *merely receptive* for the space of five minutes he would rest from the preceding class. The pure air and increased circulation of his blood freed his system of many toxins.

Rest by the right use of leisure time.[1] As we have

---

[1] The translator has thought the "change of occupation" idea, several times indicated by the author, so worth emphasizing in a place of its own that he has taken the liberty of inserting this and the following paragraph. To the reader is recommended the brilliant essay of Josef Pieper, *Leisure the Basis of Culture*, New York: Pantheon, 1952.

said before, idleness is no solution. (Doubtless you have also heard it called "the devil's workshop.") In both normal and excessive fatigue "just doing nothing" brings no real rest. A change of occupation is more restful than merely stopping work. The right use of leisure time will do much for your health, happiness, efficiency, concentration and longevity. You will become more interested and more interesting.

Manual workers should make a hobby of one of the fine arts, one of the sciences, social work, a parish activity, or investigate the world of books or new fields of knowledge. Those, on the other hand, whose work is mostly intellectual should for part of their leisure time take up some outdoor occupation or hobby which involves more or less vigorous physical exercise. If this is difficult they should at least make a hobby of some manual skill (one of the handicrafts or applied arts). Those who must work with their heads will thus gain greater benefit than by merely turning to some different field of intellectual endeavor. They should also do something with their hands.

You can rest from excessive work by engulfing yourself in studies or occupations or hobbies which amuse and interest you. In these you will easily obtain tranquil and perfect concentration. Another way is deliberately to experience some affection; for example, love of parents, brothers or sisters. This is why a mother who loves her child really rests while working for him. Acts of reverence, confidence, love of God in prayer also produce these good effects. Try to have a loving feeling of His Divine Presence everywhere, especially in yourself and your neighbors through sanctifying grace.

Bodily Relaxation

The foregoing exercises will help to avoid all mental tension. But joined with this tension or caused by it, there is another, a muscular and nervous tension in hands, feet and diaphragm, and especially in the eyes. If through proper exercises you relax these members suitably, you will experience greater mental rest.

Nervous and Muscular Rest.—Tension, worry and overexertion easily have repercussions throughout the whole nervous system, and more especially in the eyes, by putting into a state of abnormal contraction the nerves and muscles which are scarcely ever wholly relaxed even in sleep. If you relax your mind you will more easily relax those muscles. Likewise, if you let muscles and nerves go loose and limp, your mind will be relaxed and relieved. Since the soul is intimately united to the body it is logical that any modification in one will modify and influence the other.

You should then relax every muscle. Let them go limp. Begin with the forehead. This will lose its wrinkles or nervous contractions if you loosen up the eyes, letting the eyelids softly fall over them. Continue with the mouth, letting the corners curve up, not down. Loosen up the tongue (make a sagging face like a stupid person's). Let the hands fall softly and leave the fingers loose and limp. Place your foot on the ground with no extra effort. Loosen the muscles of neck, jaws, chest and abdomen. This is also an ideal exercise for inducing sleep. Gymnastic exercises and massaging can also produce this relaxation.

Resting the Vision.—The eye-ball's many nerves and accommodation muscles grow tense through worry, anxiety or mental tension. If you do not relax them before going to bed they will not loosen up at all during sleep, especially if the previous tension has been profound or prolonged. When this goes on for weeks and months they finally lose their elasticity. They will then be unable to accommodate the eye as they should. Farsightedness, nearsightedness and bad focussing will result. In order to relax them we here propose several exercises recommended by experience and by the eye-specialist, Dr. Bates.

1. Palming. Sit down comfortably and relax your whole body. Let your eyelids fall softly and close the eyes without pressure. Think of the eye-ball as soft, limp and free of tension. Think that a smile is spreading evenly throughout the closed eyes. Imagine there is no light at all in them, that everything is soft and black. Cover them with the palms of your hands. Cup your hands a little so as not to press on the eye-ball. Put your knees rather close together and lean your elbows on them. Relax the breathing muscles.

The important thing is for the eyes to be closed, well covered and as relaxed as possible. The blacker the color seen, the better relaxation and rest. Your mind should also rest at the same time. Either let it wander on pleasant subjects or imagine that the darkness is growing blacker and blacker. Ten or twenty minutes of this, two or three times a day will produce great bodily and mental rest and will sometimes alleviate and even cure farsightedness.

If you are agitated or tired at bedtime you should sacrifice a part of your sleep in order to relax your eyes. As a result you will sleep much better.

2. *Blinking.* Do this for about ten seconds. This rest nature claims spontaneously. Fixed, staring eyes are positively unnatural. This is a harmful habit and causes fatigue and tension.

3. *Cold water baths.* This relaxing effect can also be obtained by splashing a few handfuls of water on your closed eyes.

After these exercises open your eyes and take a look around. Let the vision of an object or book come to you of itself and rest within your eye. Do not, as it were, reach out after it. Effort to see hinders our seeing well.

The normal eye does not attempt to see a large amount all at the same time. Practice looking, for example, not at a whole line but at a word or phrase.

The eyes' movements are so rapid that we get the impression that they cover a great space at once. But when you try to see everything at once your eyes are in a state of tension. Relax and let them go limp if you wish to see without fatigue. In reading you should use your eyes as you do in writing. You do not then put on the pressure but watch each word as you write it. So, in reading and seeing, you should take in every detail in its own time and not be in a hurry to see the whole thing at once.

After all illnesses the eyes, too, are convalescent. In a general weakness or fatigue these too are weak. At such times you should not make them work as if they were in perfect condition. Reading is one of the most difficult tasks for the eyes. The sick should only read a little bit, or for short spaces of time. They should frequently close their eyes for a few minutes' rest. They should never make an effort to read. If you are suffering from mental or nervous fatigue you should never read without first resting for fifteen minutes of sleep or for twenty minutes with your eyes closed. Then read with your eyes relaxed. Read for only a short time at a stretch and stop for rest when you come to periods or paragraph endings.

RESTING WHILE ASLEEP

Although it is not the only way to rest, sleep is a synonym for perfect physical and mental relaxation. That is why insomnia is so annoying, especially for nervous people. Yet we can, for their direction, affirm that (1) one hour of perfect rest is worth more than two hours of rest that is imperfect or accompanied by dreams; (2) five hours of sleep are sufficient for making up for daily fatigue; (3) even if you do not sleep at all, if you stay in bed with your brain in perfect repose or in a receptive state, you will obtain a rest which is almost complete.

The head of a large college began to suffer from insomnia because of illness. At first he was a bit worried. But then he said to himself, "If I can't sleep, at least I am going to rest in bed." He went about this with perfect bodily relaxation and peace of mind. Weeks and months passed without this forcing him to give up his job. He admitted to me that for six months he could not remember having slept for a minute with total lack of consciousness. When he finally lost his fears of insomnia and no longer worried about the absence of sleep, gradually sleep began to return to him.

Sleep with dreams, and especially with nightmares, is no longer perfect repose. For the brain is then unconsciously working. This work can even cause fatigue.

Duration of sleep.—This should vary according to the age and constitution of each individual. As a general norm we can say that when the organism is in a period of development more than seven hours seems needful. Babies and little children need more than ten. Adolescents should have from eight to ten, and young people from seven to eight. For adults seven hours are recommended, although, according to noted authors and the experience of many, only five hours would be sufficient. Total satiation with sleep makes some nervous people more apt to lose control because they find it more difficult to go to sleep next time.

Dreams

The cause of dreams can be bodily (a position of the body which oppresses the heart, bad digestion, general weakness) or mental. The latter may be lack of control over the day's acts and ideas, especially those which immediately precede sleep, or studying with concomitant anxiety or parasite ideas, or strong impressions, worries and emotional conflicts.

Remedy.—Be calm and controlled for about twenty minutes before going to bed. In the case of many religious orders and congregations, Christian families or Catholic colleges, this is made easier by their night prayers or examination of conscience, or their evening visit to the church or chapel. If you awaken in the middle of a dream, you should not turn over and go back to sleep again. For you will then just go on dreaming. You should get up or thoroughly awaken yourself and by means of fully conscious acts for ten or twenty minutes cut the thread of the dream.

An afternoon nap is advisable only when it is a

truly restorative sleep, when it does not impede digestion or stop you from promptly falling asleep at night.

Insomnia

We are not speaking here of insomnia from bodily causes, from a pain in stomach or tooth, from cold or heat, but of mental insomnia. This insomnia is partial when it takes a long time to get to sleep. It is total when there is no total lack of consciousness.

The immediate physiological cause of insomnia is excitation of the sympathetic [1] nervous system. According to the most modern theories sleep is a result of harmony between the sympathetic and parasympathetic [2] nervous systems. Hence when the activity of the first which predominates in the state of wakefulness, is checked or diminished by tranquillity or relaxation, it comes into equilibrium with the activity of the second until sleep is finally produced.

In any theory, however, what produces this excitation or overactivity of the sympathetic nervous system is excessive work on the part of your produc-

---

[1] The *sympathetic* nervous system is made up of two cords, one on either side of the spinal column, and connected by nerve fibers with the external blood vessels, glands, smooth muscles, etc. One of its functions is to speed up the heart.

[2] The *parasympathetic* nervous system is made up of two groups of nerves arising in the cranial and sacral regions respectively. These have among their functions the constricting of the pupils, dilating of blood vessels, slowing of the heart and increasing the action of the glands and digestive and reproductive organs.

tive power. Today it may be an uncontrolled fixed idea, or an associated train of ideas corresponding to what you see and hear during the day. Tomorrow it may be some emotional conflict or a simple fear of the insomnia experienced before. Another time it might be an annoyingly unpleasant noise, such as another person's snoring or a neighbor's radio.

It is a big mistake to say, "Go to sleep quickly for there isn't much time." Given to a person (or to oneself) on the way to bed, this order is more likely to produce the opposite effect. Because going to sleep is an unconscious process, we make it more difficult by trying to bring the will into it. The less you think about it the better. Sleep is like your shadow; if you go after it, it flees from you.

Remedies for Insomnia

1. Eliminate previous nervous excitement.—Before going to bed calm down and control mental and nervous excitement for twenty minutes or so by means of conscious acts or clear sensations. Or voluntarily concentrate on other matters. This will prevent those memories or impressions from coming back to excite your nerves. Twenty minutes are enough to calm the greatest excitement.

Here is something which happened to me when I first received my assignment to the "Catholic Mission," Wuhu-An, China. It was something I had always desired out of supernatural motives. Yet the letter's arrival that evening made quite an impression on me. Here was a new course plotted for my whole life, a farewell to my country, its mentality, its language. I was tossing over and over in bed for an hour without being able to get to sleep. Then I remembered the remedy, got up, turned on the light and applied the method of conscious sensations. After a half hour of this exercise, I calmed down, went to bed again and fell asleep in five minutes.

2. Eliminate a fixed idea or train of ideas.—Once in bed, or just beforehand, repel this fixed idea or interrupt the train of ideas by filling your consciousness with sensations (receptive mental activity). If there is an emotional conflict discover where it is and dissolve it in the same way. When going to bed you should put up the following imaginary sign to oppose your worries or business of the day: "Closed temporarily for repairs."

3. Eliminate the subconscious fear of not sleeping. After a night or several nights of insomnia you go to bed with a fear and anxiety about not sleeping. This may also be present even when you seem to have an interior resignation. Your breathing is not entirely free or deep. Your muscular relaxation is not complete. This anxiety or fear is what is enslaving you. Even though it seems strange, the best remedy is to ask you *to will not to sleep* for a fixed length of time (one or two hours). If your decision or promise is sincere you will notice at once that the hidden anxiety is gone. The breathing which was rather short before is now more natural and deeper. Once the fear of not sleeping is gone (now that you yourself *want* not to sleep), your productive power stops working on that idea. The activity of your sympathetic nervous system diminishes, and you consequently feel the sensation of sleep coming on. But, notice, you should be faithful to your pledge and resist sleep during the time determined. Otherwise the penalty will be to make this remedy useless when another occasion arises. If the fear reappears when you try to go to sleep again, repeat the same procedure even if you have to sacrifice several hours, or a whole night or several nights. It is certain that you will win out in the end.

Do not give too much importance to sleep by thinking that a certain number of hours is indispensable. Sometimes a simple mental sleep is sufficient (making yourself merely receptive, with muscular relaxation and rhythmic breathing).

4. Eliminate the annoyance of noise.—When you find you are annoyed by a noise (another's snoring, traffic noises, the ticking of a clock, a neighbor's radio), notice that the racket is not the cause but only a condition of insomnia. For we sleep on a train with a great deal more noise going on. The immediate and true cause are the ideas which the noise awakens in us and which we do not control (indignation, impatience, anxiety to sleep). The remedy lies in willing to hear the noise. Make yourself a voluntary receiver of it, without subjectively modifying it with other ideas. The sense of hearing has sound as its proper object. It should then be able to find its satisfaction in it.

During a pilgrimage I was sharing my room with another. Hardly had he gone to bed than he began to snore loudly enough to waken the dead. At first I started to be impatient. Then I applied the remedy. I willed to listen to the snoring and hear it clearly, tranquilly observed it and a little later fell asleep. Waking up once during the night (the noise was terrific) I used the same method again and returned to sleep.

Recommended by many as a simple general method for going to sleep is the following. *Beforehand,* calm down and control yourself if there is any excitement. *On going to bed,* deliberately relax the muscles and nerves of eyes, then forehead, neck, mouth and limbs. Breathe rhythmically, deeply, and rather audibly just as a person who is already asleep. Peacefully take notice of your breathing (receptivity) without thinking about anything else. *Afterwards,* do not give too much importance to sleep. Know how to profit from relaxation and "mental" sleep.

OUTLINE DIAGRAM

How to Rest

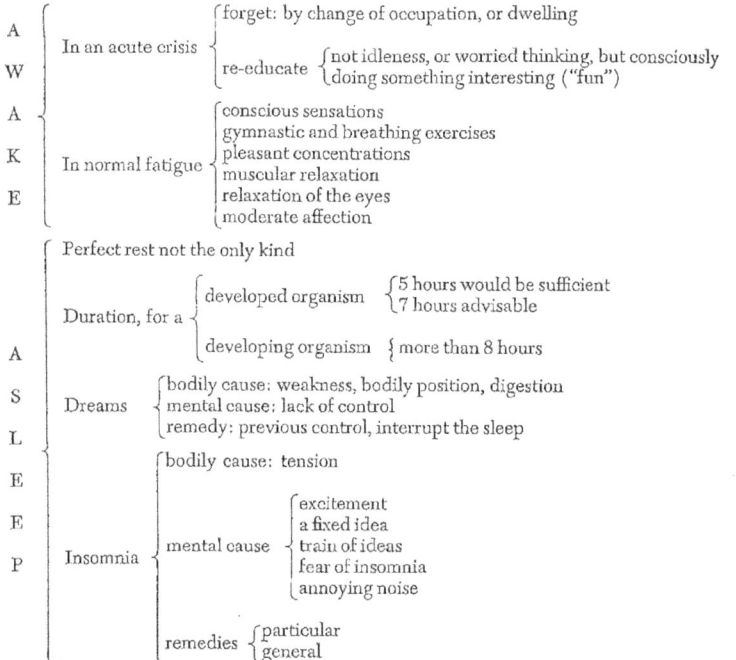

VII

How to Think

MEMORY

Your memory's function is to file away mental acts and afterwards find them. It is both library and librarian of phenomena which pass through your consciousness: sensations, images, feelings, reasoning processes and will acts.

You should file away sensations, images and acts. The more consciously these enter "by receptive attention" or through a greater number of senses (hearing, sight, touch), the more deeply will they be engraved. This is the pedagogical reason for teaching with visual aids, the theater, movies, slide films, and so forth. You should also file away ideas and reasoning processes. You can take these from books, conversations, meditations, lectures and other forms of discourse or writing. The greater attention you have, the better you will retain them in memory.

You should be able to find things. It is hard to find books in a library if they have no titles, have not been catalogued by the librarian, or have not been put in their proper place. In the same way you do not remember half-conscious ideas which come from studying or working without full concentration. On the other hand, you do remember what you have learned in a definite order, with clear connections made. And you remember more easily when you refer what you learn to other related ideas—the part with the whole, cause with its effect, and so on. Hence you should use "keys" or diagrams, synopses or resumés, well catalogued slips of paper or cards, underlining or marking with red pencil, and the like.

A French teacher used to bring to class different objects which the students would see and touch as they pronounced each object's name or the name of the action, of touching, carrying, and so forth. He had movies or slides projected which he explained in French. He played French recordings for them. A month later the pupils were able to repeat the narration of an event or explanation of a picture in the same language. Join the pleasure factor (feelings) to variety and the use of several senses.

Other Efficiency Factors

Capitalize on Your Feelings.—When you study in an atmosphere of interest your attention is easily aroused and what you learn is deeply impressed.

Convince yourself or a pupil of the ease and profit of an assignment and you have won half the battle.

Use Your Own Predominant Kind of Memory.—Visual memory is predominant in some (they remember the page or the place where they read something). If you are one of these, use the same book or notebook and write down what you see or learn. Auditory memory is predominant in others. They retain what they hear or say aloud. To this latter class belonged the famous Scripture scholar, Fr. Maldonatus, S.J. He confessed that he retained almost nothing of what he read unless he read it aloud.

Work at the Right Time.—The best time for memory work is in the early morning and at night, that is, the times nearest to sleep, nearest to unconsciousness. And you will do more in three quarters of an hour if the period is interrupted than in the same unbroken length of time. Make sure that during the interruptions you do not use your memory for learning other things.

UNDERSTANDING

Your talent or aptitude for study is in direct proportion to your ease of concentration and ability to see relationships. Because of brain structure or special instruction some can do this easily, others cannot. Teach yourself or a pupil to concentrate and to see the relationship or connection between ideas.

This is the secret both of pedagogy and success in studies.

At college there was a man in my year who, whenever he studied mathematics, abstracted from everything else. His concentration was so profound that even when bells rang he paid no attention at all to any other thing for four or six hours. He had truly extraordinary powers of concentration. Later on he was among the best students at the University of Madrid.

On the other hand I had a pupil who, though he did not waste a minute of his study time, was always the last in his class. I called him aside and questioned him on his methods of study. He would distractedly read and reread the lesson without understanding it. He was always trying to learn by brute memory. He did not know how to concentrate. I taught him to read the first paragraph with attention, and summarize it in a few words, then the second and third, relating these to the first. Thus he learned to concentrate little by little and see the relationship between the summaries he made. And he finally completed his studies satisfactorily.

Remedies for Lack of Concentration.—Deficient concentration is just another name for mental wandering. This may be mere neglect to fix the attention, or may be caused by almost continual distractions either when you are studying or through the whole day. To remedy this insist on the following means.

(1) Foster conscious life (receptivity). Multiply fully conscious sensations and acts during the day.

(2) Re-educate concentration by the exercises in chapter II.

(3) Make acts of the will. Focus these upon study and progress, beginning with easy acts and advancing to the more difficult. For instance, *will* to concentrate your attention on a paragraph or half page. Or *will* to listen attentively for five, ten or fifteen minutes to reading or a lecture. Do this several times a day.

(4) Accustom yourself to read and summarize in writing. First do the first paragraph, then the second, and so on. In general this is the best method. And should you object that in this way you will never finish the lesson or book, I answer with the Latins, *"Festinabis lente."* By going slowly you will soon get there, for you do not have to read the lesson many times.

(5) Bring in your feelings. Desire, for example, will reinforce your attention. Consider the fittingness, utility or ease of your studies. Or allow yourself a moderate fear of the examination or failure. (If fear is excessive, it will prevent concentration. See below.)

Lack of Concentration Caused by Obsessing Ideas.— Vices, sinful relationships, worries, scruples and phobias, if they are very strong, end up by making all concentration impossible. One young man finished up a year in a Jesuit college brilliantly. His father was delighted and to reward him gave him every opportunity for illicit pleasure during vacation. Next year he was last in the class. To stimulate him one of his professors said, "Last year you were first in the class, but now . . ." "Father," the young man replied with tears, "I lived like a pig during the vacation and now I can think about nothing else."

And so it is necessary to tear out by the roots voluntary causes of obsessions. This is done by overcoming the emotional conflict between the higher level of mental activity and the lower levels which are so sensitive to sense pleasure and feelings. Do this by means of the Sacrament of Penance or by the methods indicated in chapters IV and IX.

Lack of Concentration from Fear of Fatigue.—Those who have to interrupt their studies or work because of mental fatigue are easily impressed by this feeling of fear. When they want to take up their work again the thought comes to them, "I can work for fifteen or twenty minutes without fatigue but no more." And when this time has passed they really begin to feel tired, to have a burning forehead, and so on. However, this feeling of fatigue is not produced by the work. It comes from lack of concentration. The parasite idea of fear of fatigue arises when they think they have passed their limit. The remedy is to belittle the discomfort and fatigue and persuade yourself that it is possible to increase your study time by ten minutes without fatigue. Then go at it without worry or fear. Little by little you can prolong this time until you finally reach normal capacity again.

One young student could not read or write for more than fifteen minutes without feeling great fatigue. Then his father died. The sad news afflicted him no little. But his religious feelings brought him great consolation. He was unable to return home and console his mother and brothers, so did this by letter. He wrote eight long pages in an hour and a half without becoming tired. The intense feeling of sorrow and family affection brought him perfect concentration on that occasion. It annihilated or repressed his habitual fear of fatigue.

Efficiency Factors

Study Relationships.—Relate the effect to the cause, the part to the whole, the first paragraph to the second, the summaries to one another. Use keys and diagrams which give a bird's-eye view. See the whole thing as a unit. Then the parts themselves will make a deeper impression on you.

Vary Your Study.—Scientific research has successfully worked on the assumption that different brain areas function for different subject matters and different mental activities. Hence the way to avoid fatigue or saturation in one specific matter will be to alternate science and literature, reading and writing, study and prayer, work with your head and work with your hands, and so on.

You can better stand the work of composing or copying if while writing you are merely receptive. Follow the movement of the pen or touch of the typewriter keys. The time for thinking or editing will be the moment of production or work. And the time of writing will be for reception or rest. Thus you will also avoid the mistakes or "slips of the pen" which come from the overlapping of two ideas. One idea is what you were just thinking about. This guides the act of writing almost subconsciously. The other idea (a parasite idea) is the one which struggles to gain the center of consciousness as you write.

Study in Peace.—Never predetermine a definite amount of work for a definite time, especially if the time be short. For this would give rise to worry and hurry to finish. Your work would be accompanied by a parasite idea. This is the reason why so many students just before their examinations tire out their heads by wanting to finish a great deal of matter in a short time. This fatigue is sometimes rather lasting in its effects. Then they cannot give a good account of what they really know because of a confusion of obscure ideas.

Study under the Right Bodily Conditions.—Avoid studying when you are physically weak, on an empty stomach, during convalescence, when exhausted or after excessive bodily fatigue. During the process of full digestion, also, mental work is less efficient and can be harmful. For when the stomach is in full activity and the blood is rushing to its aid, your brain has a smaller supply of blood and is consequently less prepared for work. If you send a rush of blood to your head by concentration, you make digestion more difficult. The old proverb has truth in it: "After dinner don't even read the address on an envelope."

Each week while still suffering from mental fatigue, I used to take a fifteen-mile walk in the space of six hours. Returning home after such a long mental rest, I thought I would take up my books to study. But I would soon have to put them aside. Without knowing it the body's exhaustion was influencing my mental powers.

PRAYER

Prayer without distractions is very consoling, enlivening and solidly educational. But if you are uncontrolled, tired or nervous, you cannot demand an hour or even a half hour of meditation or vocal prayer from yourself without continual mental wandering. However, you can attain better attention through the training explained in the first part of this book, and by bringing will acts into your prayer.

Practice.—I plan to say the Rosary, Litanies, and such like prayers without distractions. If before beginning I try to make an act of the will "not to be distracted for the whole time," I shall find it hard even to feel the possibility of this. Hence I shall make only an ineffectual desire. But if I make it more concrete and, for example, say, "During the *Kyries* I want to feel humility," or "During the first *Our Father* I want to feel confidence," I shall realize the possibility of this. The act of will will be a true one and consequently effective. As a matter of fact I really will have attention and that feeling for the first few moments. It will afterwards be easier to prolong these through the rest of my prayer.

This work of making the mental acts of prayer concrete is what St. Ignatius with masterly psychology teaches us to do in the "points" for meditation. Thereby we anticipate the first few considerations and will acts, and close the door to distractions.

Affective Prayer.—When we have the feeling for prayer (psychologically speaking, when it is pleasurable), then we have true concentration. This type of concentration hardly fatigues us at all. And so if you are tired, you can obtain sufficient attention in prayer by dwelling on appropriate feelings or will acts.

Consider the following example: I am going to meditate on the Cross of Christ. I shall ask Him, "Lord, when You were hanging on the Cross, did You suffer much?" After listening to the answer, affirmative and in detail, I shall arouse a feeling of compassion and repeat twenty or thirty times, "Lord, were you thinking about me?" On hearing that He did think of my sins and paid the penalty for them,

I shall let myself be dominated by the feeling of gratitude to Jesus Christ and hatred of sin. Then I shall summarize this attitude in a phrase, repeat it many times, varying its wording now and again, and end with a concrete act of the will (some plan to be carried out that very day). "Lord, what were You thinking and expecting of me?" "That by following My example you would love suffering and poverty, and thus store up treasure in Heaven." Another repeated affection, plan, and so forth.

In this or a similar way you can persevere easily in a half-hour or hour of prayer. It will be very profitable, consoling, and strengthening. And there need be no distractions or mental fatigue. St. Ignatius Loyola teaches us that it is not much knowledge that fills and satisfies the soul but tasting and feeling things interiorly.

OUTLINE DIAGRAM

How to Think

MEMORY	It should file away		images and acts—by receptive attention ideas and reasoning processes—by perfect concentration and do this with pleasure—by using the feelings use your predominant kind of memory work at the right time
	It should be able to find things		not semiconscious or distracted acts but arranged in order and with connections resumés and keys
UNDERSTANDING	Attention difficult because of	Mental wandering: educate yourself by	receptivity concentration exercises will acts resumés desire or moderate fear
		obsessing ideas	root out vices dissolve conflicts
		fear of fatigue	study without fearing fatigue gradual increase of time belittle the fatigue
	Efficiency factors	relate	cause and effect use diagrams
		vary	the matter: science, literature reading, writing work with head, with hands
		calm procedure—do not predetermine the amount of time or work	
		with the right bodily conditions	not when exhausted nor on an empty stomach nor after a full meal
PRAYER	Without distraction or fatigue	difficult when tired	
		easy	by re-education with an act of the will added in affective prayer

VIII

How to USE the Will

IRRATIONAL ANIMALS come perfect from the hand of the Creator. By merely following their instincts they develop and reach their goal. They have no need of education. But man is born incomplete. If he follows his animal instinct alone he weakens himself, sickens and dies. For this reason God gives him reason, first that of his parents and teachers, then afterwards his own. God says to him, "Complete yourself." Man's duty then will always be to perfect himself, educate, complete and gain the mastery of himself.

The need for education is founded in the struggle between the lower level of mental activity and the higher. The lower level has an appetite only for sense goods, even to the prejudice of higher goods. The higher level of mental activity is capable of knowing and attaining higher goods which are beyond normal sensible experience, are true and eternal. These are goods of the soul, social goods and divine goods.

THE WILL AND MENTAL ACTIVITY

As a compass (or sort of gun-sight) for direction in your own education or that of another, keep in mind these two principles: (1) intense mental acts remain behind within us, and (2) there is a triple scale of values in normal mental activity.

The Persistence of Mental Acts

Every intense mental act contributes to formation or deformation of personality or character. It remains associated with acts which preceded it. Even though unconscious or forgotten, it continues to influence your personality by making related acts more easy and contrary ones more difficult. For the same reason virtues practised in childhood or at any other time will form within your personality a definite framework of mind. By this you are more apt to act well and efficiently than if this practice had never existed. Likewise a transgression or concession to exaggerated instincts, even if made only once and during youthful folly and even with a resolve to return straightway to the right road, will leave forever within your mental framework a greater inclination to evil and less ease in doing good. A single fault or passing sin is then of no little importance. This is true even though it later incurs no penalty. Nor is any act of virtue unimportant even if it is hidden or unrewarded.

Triple Scale of Values in Normal Mental Activity

The Whole Should Prevail over the Part.—Partial tendencies must be subordinated to the activity of the whole. The special difficulty here arises from the following.

(1) You are dependent on matter as regards food, rest and bodily appetites. These must be brought into harmony with the spirituality of the soul. (Hence follow temperance, chastity, and so forth.)

(2) Many processes in you are almost mechanical even though you do possess a higher liberty.

(3) The course of your thinking is fantastic when under the influence of emotion. This will sometimes be so even despite your thirst for objective truth. (There is a dominion of imagination, exaggerated fears and feelings.)

What is Objective and Real Should Prevail over What is Subjective.—In the beginning a child lives enclosed in his own personality. He does not want to do service or give himself. He is an egoist, merely subjective. Normal development or education will bring him to the recognition and realization of objective and social values. He will then make them his norm of action. From his social isolation he will lean towards whoever offers him support. He will want to change himself into a useful and working member of the community. Only a morbid mental pattern will make a man an egoist.

Development Should be Continuous.—Your whole being tends to develop progressively, become the master of itself, realize its ideal gradually.

You may draw important ascetical conclusions from these principles. (1) If you give up self-conquest and mortification as a means of rising from vice or sin, there will be a regression in your development or progress. (2) The "liberation of your personality toward objective values" (that is, society or God) is in psychology what in asceticism is called self-conquest, humility or charity. The false asceticisms—stoicism, buddhism, spiritism, laicism—all insist upon partial dispositions. They point you toward a closed personality rather than toward an open one as in Christianity. They can as a result turn you aside to morbid and perverse forms of asceticism. But objective and total asceticism is in harmony with normal mental life.

By education you orientate and strengthen your mind in order that it might always tend toward its own higher goods easily, freely and efficiently. To this end you must educate your will.

EDUCATION OF THE WILL BY MOTIVES[1]

Your will is a rational faculty, naturally inclined to the good. Before acting your understanding must precede it like a torchbearer and show it a good, a

---

[1] See J. Lindworsky, S.J., *Training of the Will*, Bruce, Milwaukee, 1938; and by the same author, *The Psychology of Asceticism*, Newman, Westminster, Md., 1950.

motive, a value. Then it will move into action. You should, then, propose goods or values to yourself or those whom you are to educate. These values must not only be objectively such but must be comprehended by the subject (that is, by you) as worthwhile at the present moment. In short, they must be objective, subjective and actual.

Objective Values.—These are real values, good in themselves; for example, what is useful, honorable, pleasant, necessary. These may be sensory goods perceived by the senses, or spiritual goods grasped by the understanding. They may be goods for time or eternity, partial or total goods, natural or supernatural.

Subjective Values.—These you perceive to be such. They are accommodated to your capacity. In children because of their undeveloped understanding these will be largely sensible goods or those with a sensible element. In adolescents and adults they should also be spiritual, more than merely material goods, and supernatural. But they should as far as possible be reinforced by the imagination and feelings.

The father of a family once told me, "For a long time I could not succeed in getting my three year old son to stop slamming the door. He did not understand the motive (that the noise might bother other people). But one day I gave him another reason which he did understand, 'The door is going to break.' From then on he would neither slam it himself nor let anyone else do so. He went around repeating the motive as he understood it."

Actual Values.—These are the ones found actually present in your mind at the moment of decision and execution. To keep them present it will help to write down your good resolutions and their motives. Then read them over again from time to time. For lack of this continued motivation there are very frequent failures in school and home. Children who went to Mass for years, even daily Mass, sometimes do not go at all later on when they are older. The reason is that they went before not because of any motive of their own, but because of their educators. They did not themselves make an act of the will to go to Mass. In short, the motives were not present when the time came for action.

EDUCATION OF THE WILL BY ACTION

In all languages there are two words which are magnificent, ennobling and creative: "Yes" and "No." Know how to say, "Yes" when you are going forward with great strides, and also when you are moving on an uphill road, very slowly yet ever onward. Know how to say, "No" without concessions, discussion or wavering. Herein lies growth and strength.

Active Education for Those with Loss of Will Power. —If you do not perform true will acts you will scarcely have any idea of them. What you need above all is an internal experience and intimate feeling of these acts. You must then exercise yourself in external acts which require little effort but are mentally perfect. You must make them concrete, feel their possibility, and produce the mental energy needed for decision.

Active Education for All.—You will find it very useful (1) to distinguish true acts of the will from what are not (mere desire, impulse, velleity or vague intention). (2) Make them concrete so as not to be content with a mere desire or plan. (3) Pass gradually from the easy to the difficult so as to feel their possibility, avoid failures (or false acts of the will) and discouragement.

You can also dramatize your will process by considering it as a battle and distinguishing these four stages in it.

(1) *Presentation of the contestants:* what are the acts I can will or reject? That is, stay in bed when I am called or jump out of it?

(2) *Struggle between the contestants:* discussion of motives for and against. What good or harm does staying there bring me, and what advantages are there in jumping out?

(3) *You can give the victory to whichever one you choose:* feel the possibility of this.

(4) *Victory of one over the other:* leave it as master of the field of consciousness. Imagine with concrete details how you will jump out. Banish the very thought of a possibility of staying in bed (making it impossible for yourself by decision).

The education of the will should not be just a "lighthouse education" which tries only to avoid shipwreck on the reefs and shoals of opportunity for evil. Nor should it be a merely negative one which is content to correct defects. Far better will be a positive type of education which will always propose some progress to be attained, perfections to be acquired, virtues to be practised. This provides an increase of joy, enthusiasm and sense of value. *Education lies not so much in making people put what is good into practice as in teaching them to will it and practice it under their own power.*

I had a student who was really good deep down but whose will was very weak and vacillating. He was always being punished. I asked him why he made no effort to correct himself. "I want to, Father, but I can't." I examined his act of will. He did not make it concrete or feel the possibility of it. To help him keep silence at the proper times I proposed that he bite his tongue (lightly of course) on the way from recreation to study, from study to the classroom or lecture hall. "Can you do that?" "Yes, Father." By making the thing concrete and feeling its possibility he did make definite will acts, one day to please me, another to honor the Blessed Virgin, or to please Our Lord. At night I would ask him, "How many times did you fail?" "Eight." "Then kiss the Crucifix eight times and promise not to fail tomorrow." The result was a rapid improvement which was joyful and complete.

THE IGNATIAN METHOD

The Protestant Dr. Vittoz had a great admiration for St. Ignatius Loyola. He believed that Loyola was three centuries ahead of his time in the fine introspection and effective pedagogy revealed in his *Exercises* and *Examens*. The purpose of St. Ignatius is to make a man perfect. He proceeds according to the most sublime laws of our higher mental activity without allowing the lower levels of activity or disordered feelings to disturb this process. This is indicated in the very first paragraph of his little book.[1] To this end he uses the will's legislative power in the *Exercises* to choose and determine a concrete way of life. In the *Examens* he uses the will's executive power to bring this down into practice.

The *Exercises* propose motives which are most strong and noble in themselves and which are reinforced by the feeling of love for Jesus Christ. These motives are to be subjectively felt and adopted by the exercitant. When his higher mental activity has been so directed that passions do not deroute it, then

---

[1] ". . . just as walking and running are bodily exercises, so also any method of preparing and disposing the soul to remove from itself all disordered affections (feelings and impulses) and then to seek and find the divine will in arranging one's life with a view to the soul's salvation, these are called spiritual exercises."—". . . *sicut ambulare . . . et currere sunt exercitia corporalia, ita etiam quilibet methodus praeparandi et disponendi animan ad tollendas a se omnes affectiones inordinatas, et . . . ad quaerendam, et inveniendam vóluntatem divinam, in vitae suae dispositione, ad salutem animae, vocantur exercitia spiritualia.*"—*Exercitia Spiritualia, op. cit.*, pp. 10-12.

come meditations preparatory to the "Election" (or choice of a way of life). And then come decisions about concrete details of the future way of life.

The executive power of the will has a very efficient instrument in the "particular examen." This is truly a control and stimulus to the will. The particular examen makes us perform true will acts by making them concrete, each the subject of some one virtue or vice, and in a determined place and time. It makes us feel their possibility and facility by limiting the expenditure of energy and vigilance to a half day at a time. Finally it makes us renew our decision three times a day, and strengthen it by comparison of one examen with another, with contrition when we fail and with love of Jesus Christ. *It is a spiritual treatment which is most efficacious for curing moral illnesses.*

Dr. Schleich, a Protestant, professor of the Faculty of Medicine at Berlin, asserts even more. "I say with all assurance and conviction that with these norms and exercises in our hands we could even today transform our asylums, prisons and mental institutions, and prevent the commitment to them of two thirds of the people who are today within their walls."

And so we see that the will is man's conquest of himself, and the education of the will is the strategy of this conquest.

OUTLINE DIAGRAM

How to Use the Will

- **Education necessary**
  - we are born incomplete
  - the conflict of our instincts

- **Remember for orientation**
  - intense experiences remain
  - triple scale of values
    - whole over the part
    - objective over subjective
    - development continuous

- **Educate the will**
  - **By motives**
    - propose goods to be attained (motives)
    - *objective* (goods in themselves)
      - sensible
      - spiritual
      - eternal
    - *subjective* (perceived as such)
      - in childhood, first through the senses,
      - later in the supernatural
    - *actual*—actually present
      - when making a decision
      - when carrying it out
      - in continued motivation
  - **Actively**
    - for the abulic
      - internal experience of will act
      - practice easy external acts
    - for everyone
      - distinguish will act from mere desire, impulse, etc.
      - progress gradually to more difficult acts
      - dramatize the will process
      - action under one's own power
  - **Ignatian method**
    - legislative power of will in the *Exercises*
      - choice in light of great motives
      - choice made concrete in *Election*
    - executive power of will in the *particular examen*
      - concrete
        - some one virtue or vice
        - in definite place
        - at determined time
      - possibility felt
        - half day at a time
        - renewals of decision
        - thrice daily

IX

How to Control Feelings

FEELING IS A FORCE God gives you for willing and working with greater energy and constancy. But like steam in a locomotive it is a chaotic force. If well channeled by reason (with its safety valves and opportune expansion and release) it will be exceedingly useful to you.

GENERAL CONTROL

Do Not Let Feelings Govern You

Make no change under the influence of feelings. To have as a norm of action "because I like to" is the same as to take a trolley car or bus without bothering about where it is going or only because it is more comfortable or is shinier than another. Likewise, to stop working "because it is a bother" or "troublesome," is to renounce success, joy, glory and even your own salvation.

> *To want something only because there is no other way out, is the way a slave acts.*
>
> *To want it because it is no trouble (following likes or impulses) is the way an animal acts.*
>
> *To want it in spite of the bother (guided by reason or duty) is the way a rational human being acts.*
>
> *To want even the bother of it (with your eyes on the ideal or on God) is the way a hero or saint acts.*

The child and the socially unadapted person love or hate, work or stop working only because of their likes and dislikes, because reason has not been developed or has been inhibited.

Govern Your Feelings

Restrain exaggeration of feelings. Do not give too much importance to them, or to what pleases or displeases you, or to what you fear or desire. For experience tells us that feeling heightens colors, exaggerates good or evil, obscures and alters truth.

For example, do the words or behaviour of another irritate you? Then your feelings will make you tend to think that he has a deliberate bad intention (whereas he probably only acted out of lightmindedness, or without full reflection). They will even persuade you that he has yet worse plans for the future. Does the mailman or telegraph messenger bring you bad news? At least your imagination will immediately run riot and overload the unopened envelope with the blackest shadows. "Somebody is dead," you may think. Or, "Some relative has gone bankrupt." Do you feel a little unwell? Your uncontrolled thought will tell you, "It must be tuberculosis or heart trouble or the beginnings of insanity." Is it a case of not making progress in your studies, or in virtue or prayer? Do you find yourself sad and discouraged and wish to give up the spiritual life you adopted? Does it seem to you that you were not made for this? *In all these cases you have lost control of your feelings.*

Control Your Thoughts

Do not give free rein to their deceptive arguments. Avoid their exaggerations and transfers to other fields. Think about something else and, above all, *do not change your plans or make important resolutions under the sway of feeling*. Let a day go by. Let a night go by too. "Consult your pillow." Then when your feelings are calmed you will be disposed for work and you will see that "the lion is not so fierce as he is painted."

With his fine sense of psychology St. Ignatius traces out for us three very wise rules for governing ourselves when a depressing feeling comes over us.

Firstly, in time of desolation (that is, when you are discouraged or sad, without light or strength, without peace or consolation, or when temptation blinds you) make no change but continue with the plans you made when you had peace, light and consolation.

Secondly, think of the fact that this state will pass and that light and joy will return. Encourage the thoughts and feelings you had before the desolation came.

Thirdly, act against the very desolation. Do the opposite of what you feel yourself inclined to do. Lengthen your prayer, for example, or perform even more mortifications.

In the Palace of Feelings there are brilliant halls where dwell optimism, hope, love, valor and joy. And there are dark cellars, lurking places of discouragement, sadness, fear, worry, anger. The mistress of the Palace, the will, has to pass through all its rooms but can delay wherever she wishes. We should not give too much importance to fears or sadness when they come. We should not habitually and voluntarily stay with them, but pass on to the halls of joy and optimism.

Open the Safety Valve

There are states of feeling in which repression can cause fatigue, suffering and illness. Such are the apparent conflicts between the commands of duty and the demands of honor, love or instinct. Frequently the mere manifestation of these to your mental guide or spiritual director will lighten them, reveal the solution and cure them.

HOW TO CONTROL FEELINGS

During the first World War psychiatrists were surprised to note the greater number of cases of severe mental illness among English soldiers than among the French. They investigated the causes and found that the former had been brought up in the atmosphere of believing that an Englishman should not feel fear and that it would be a national disgrace to give any sign of it. This mentality imposed on many individuals a violent struggle, repression of unavoidable feelings, and finally mental disequilibrium. When this mentality was modified there were fewer victims.

There are four kinds of difficulties or internal conflicts which we should make known as soon as possible to a prudent director lest they poison our wills or at least tire our minds unnecessarily.

(1) *Acts* which weigh down our conscience with moral responsibility.

(2) *Worrisome practical doubts* which we cannot solve, or obsessing temptations to evil.

(3) *Tormenting indecision* in important matters (this may be a result of the preceding).

(4) *Oppressing fears or sadness* which we do not know how to control.

When a tumor is opened, the victim is relieved. So a release of these emotional conflicts with a prudent friend or spiritual guide, and above all the divine release of them in sacramental Confession, roots out of our soul all that poisonous overload. It brings us so much peace, joy and encouragement that non-Catholic doctors of different countries agree that if Confession had not been established in the Church as a spiritual medicine, they would have had to prescribe it themselves as a treatment for emotional ailments rising from disordered feelings.

You should also open the safety valve of dignified affection in the expansions of family love, true friendship, spiritual confidences, love of your neighbor, love of souls, and love of God. All your mental energy does not flow into the channel of your understanding when you try to close off or block up the channel of feeling. There must be some release of feeling.

Close the Escape Valve to Brute Instinct and Disordered Passions

A fourth year medical student once came to see me after a lecture. He could not sleep, study or fix his attention. He was wallowing in discouragement, depression and profound sadness. He had to stop attending classes. He had been studying intensely, at the same time had to attend to troublesome family affairs, and was also worrying about an illness of his father's. He consulted an atheistic psychiatrist who recommended certain injections which would afford a release to his sexual instinct. This latter, according to the diagnosis, was being repressed and was the cause of his illness. The young man followed this foolish advice only to find himself even more confused, sad and worried. Once the true cause of his sickness was found and all was made right with God through Confession, he began the work of re-education joyfully. He recovered his ability to sleep in two days.

Apparently there are not a few atheistic psychiatrists who follow Freud (as they say) and want to re-establish lost equilibrium by subjecting the angel to the brute, the soul to the body, the higher mental activities to the lower, the conscious to the unconscious. Dr. Vittoz and his whole school, together with all spiritual psychiatrists, are in revolt against such an aberration.

You should also do away with useless confidences which are born of emotionalism or impulse. Never recount to any person you meet, just to console yourself, what you suffer or fear, desire or plan. This might give you some momentary consolation (that of yielding to the impulse) but the sad ideas will impress you more in the telling and make you more their slave. If you tell them to your friends you make them sad, if to your enemies you make them glad. The ills of another, and much less the details of what you suffer, feel or fear, are not of much interest to anyone even though his charity or courtesy lead you to think so. On the other hand, if you forget yourself in the affairs of other people you will at the same time get your own feelings under control, learn something useful, and acquire an affable and sympathetic personality.

Control Impatience

"If you have an enemy," says Dr. Fosdick, "or dislike someone, the greatest evil you can do, not to him but yourself, is to allow hatred to sink into your soul and plough a lasting furrow there."

To control the emotion of anger it will be helpful to know its psycho-physiological trajectory. Here we shall diagram only its controllable or voluntary phase, referring the reader to Chapter IV for the diagram of the first or spontaneous phase. Here we are using *anger* as a concrete illustration of the growth and flowering of emotions and feelings.

A. Spontaneous Phase

Injustice, insults, or annoyances affect the cerebral cortex by means of the senses or imagination. If we perceive these as contrary to our life, honor, health or ideals, we form one of the three following judgments.

"I, They, It"

I: "With my good qualities, merits, and intentions, I do not deserve such treatment."

They: "They are unfair, cruel, ungrateful, or unbearable."

It: "It [the event] is unfair, unjust, intolerable, dangerous."

Especially if it is very prolonged and is felt to be very strong, this concrete judgment stimulates the hypothalamus which is the engine room of the emotions. Thence the autonomic nervous system spontaneously goes into action. This, plus the action of adrenalin, puts heart, stomach, lungs, muscles, viscera, etc. in hyperactivity. And we are invaded by feelings of disgust and antipathy.

This is an example of what the classical moral philosophers and moral theologians call *motus primo primi*. In it there is no responsibility nor any sin. We really cannot control it except indirectly, and then only with a great deal of vigilance. We can try to avoid the exciting factor, or at least the memory of it, and to shorten its duration. We do find that we are able to avoid making the concrete judgment, "I, They, It", or at least to modify it once it is present in us. This we can do either by deliberately interposing a distraction or, better, by deliberately forming in ourselves a different attitude by means of an adequate education or re-education. If we do this the disturbance will pass rather quickly without leaving behind a lasting or profound effect.

B. Voluntary Phase

I. Destructive Development.

These disturbances in the organs themselves affect the cerebral cortex and warn us that we are beginning to be annoyed. The original stimulus itself may also be continuing to solicit our emotions. If the will, which could have distracted our attention to other things, gives in to anger, we will retain the concrete judgment, "I, They, It". This judgment will become stronger and more prolonged and will prepare us for attack or some other reaction.

The reaction may be wholly unrestrained, in which case the hypothalamus will develop an *animal wrath*

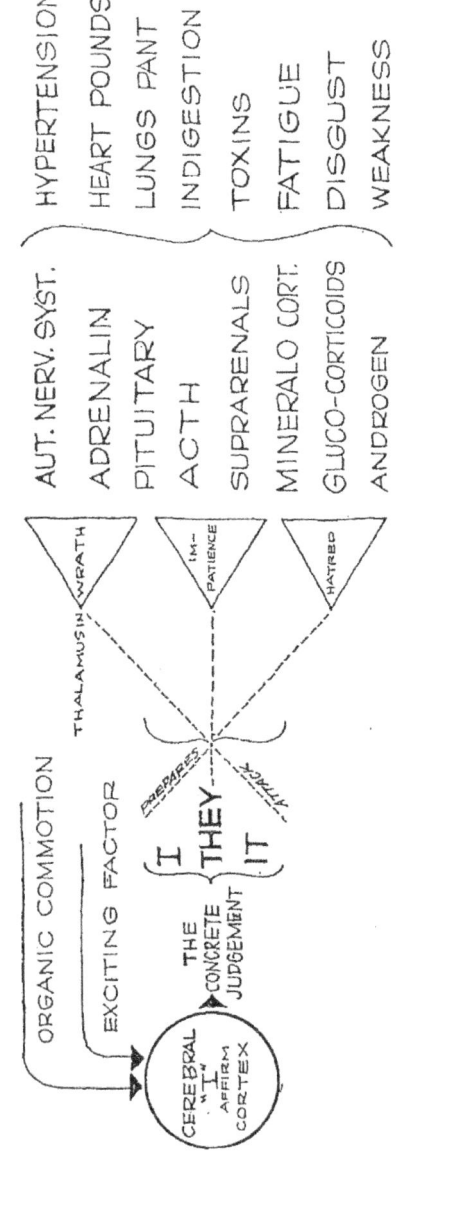

or unrestrained anger with primitive animal reactions. Or perhaps, faced with social conventions or fear of reprisals, we will be content with a restrained attack, that is to say, with a corroding *impatience* which will be accompanied by threats, or by acts which annoy our adversary, or by a feeling of disgust or sadness. Or finally, we may resolve to postpone the attack, on which occasion we conceive *hatred* or "bottled wrath" together with tension and prolonged inner disturbances.

In all of these three states the organism calls all its reserves into battle: the overexcited autonomic nervous system, the adrenalin which flows in the bloodstream and activates all the organs, the pituitary gland which liberates the hormone ACTH. This latter stimulates the suprarenal glands where there are manufactured what we might call the Atomic Bombs of the organism, sc. the groups of hormones which affect mineral metabolism, gluco-metabolism, and androgen. All these help to produce a revolution or overexcitation which is more sustained than that of the nervous system, but which liberates an enormous amount of energy as if for use in an emergency.

Moreover, the medulla of the suprarenal glands produces adrenalin which then stimulates even more the hypothalamus and the pituitary gland. Then we begin to feel the effects of hypertension in the circulatory system and musculature, the heart pounds, and the lungs labor as if to obtain more oxygen. The stomach contracts, thus stopping or disturbing the process of digestion. The whole organism becomes poisoned if anger is prolonged, and then fatigue and disgust invade us. After the emotion has passed, our resistance is weakened and we become depressed at feeling ourselves conquered by the emotion. Sometimes, too, there may come upon us an unholy joy at seeing an adversary suffer. But all these evils can be avoided by controlling the concrete judgment and by making anger subordinate to reason rather than to passion. Otherwise there are results such as in a New Orleans clinic where 76% of the patients were found to be there because of anger, hatred, or impatience, mixed with fear or anxiety.

II. Victorious Development.

When the signals of an emotional disturbance come to the cerebral cortex, we notice that we are becoming annoyed and that our organism is beginning to prepare itself for attack or defense. The stimulus itself, the injury or the memory of one, may still be exciting us also. Then, instead of letting ourselves be dominated by the emotion, if we order that it be controlled, the free will can follow either or both of two procedures.

First, it can modify the concrete judgment, "I, They, It" either by weakening it through a distraction or, better, annihilating it by a contrary judgment.

Secondly, it can order the contrary internal attitude of love and sympathy and the external expression of this on the face, in the tone of voice, and in muscular activity.

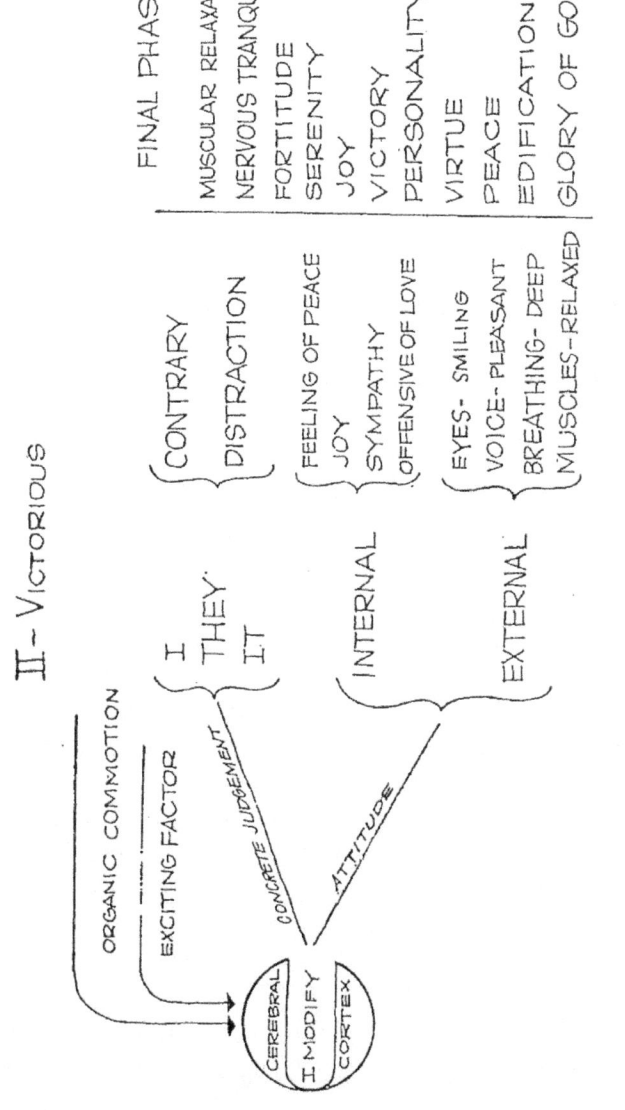

1. Control by means of distraction.

"Every morning," says the Doctor of Gentleness, St. Francis de Sales, "prepare your soul for a tranquil day." When you are at peace foster this advantageous state for the sake of your own advancement. Continually exercise yourself in acts of goodness and gentleness. If something bothers you, do not be disturbed or resist it. But when it comes, humble yourself graciously in the presence of God and try to put your soul into a tranquil state. Say, "Yes, I stumbled there; I must be more careful." Do this always, however often you fail. Wait, have patience, gather your forces and you shall win the spirit of peace and gentleness.

We have often heard this advice given, "Calm down, don't answer, control yourself, have patience." It would be more effective if, instead of wanting to remove the feeling (which is an effect of ideas), we were to remove or modify the ideas which cause it. When another insults you or his conduct disgusts you, instead of thinking about the injustice or grossness of his behaviour, concentrate your attention on something else, objects or colors before you, or the sound waves coming at you from all directions, or (if you are a psychologist) in observing his waste of energy, his attitudes and reactions. You would then hardly feel any commotion.

2. Control by means of the contrary idea.

(1) Discover which of the three, "I, They, It" predominates in you and formulate the contrary of it.

(2) To the thought of pride or fear which the emotion arouses, e.g., "I do not deserve this treatment," oppose the following, "I am a man like others, with limitations, defects and transgressions which would deserve a greater punishment."

Instead of the idea that "They are unjust or cruel," insist on what experience teaches, namely that "Everyone has lesser defects and greater virtues than we tend to admit when we are angry." Or, "They must have done that without thinking of what they were doing, or at least there was no bad will there." Jesus Christ on the Cross used this means when He asked pardon for those who crucified and insulted Him, saying that their guilt was less because "they know not what they do."

(3) If you are a spiritual man, a Christian with a living faith, reflect that an insult is what you deserve because of your sins. Think that it is a great opportunity offered you by God to gain by a minute's patience and humiliation "an eternal reward of glory."

A Sister of Charity was once begging alms for her orphans. "An alms?" answered an anticlerical, "To support you in idleness and help enslave those kids? This is what you need." And he struck her. The Sister thought for a moment about her sins and replied without a change of countenance, "That was for me, sir. Now, something for my orphans." The man's anger vanished; he asked her pardon and gave her a substantial donation.

If the mere presence of that good person for whom

you have an aversion draws a curl to your lip and brings you a thousand sharp thoughts and words, do a bit of spiritual gymnastics and meditate on his virtues. See in him "Jesus Christ disguised in his defects," Who draws near to you that you may smile on Him, love Him, speak to Him, and serve Him with greater merit. Our Divine Master said, "As long as you did it for one of these, the least of my brethren, you did it for Me."

[4] Finally, the event itself, the "It," is not too unbearable nor too dangerous. If it deprives us of some earthly good or convenience or comfort, yet this and all the goods of the world are no more than an insignificant speck of dust in comparison to the everlasting goods which are prepared as the reward of our suffering. "Although it be encircled with thorns, it is a diamond for heaven." Injury or insult is an incendiary explosion which can only be triggered and detonated by our thoughts of protest. (At the end of Chapter XI you will find some examples of thoughts for changing sorrow into joy.)

3. *Control by means of the contrary feeling.*

We must try to substitute feelings of joy, peace, and sympathy for the feeling of disgust, perturbation, or antipathy which our emotions would tend to arouse in us. Above all we must digest inevitable suffering by accepting it fully, if we wish it not to go on poisoning us. We must treat persons *as if* they were very congenial and sympathetic. We must try to understand and value their virtues and excuse their defects. We must use a tone of respectful affection, pay them deference and do them services, pray and sacrifice for them. A month of this treatment will be enough to make us congenial and sympathetic ourselves. For knowing how to think well of others and how to smile on them is the secret of multiplying friends.

Bandits once attacked the house of a colleague of mine in China. He received their chiefs with all courtesy and kindness, just as he would orderly and more advanced people. He invited them to tea, candy and cigarettes in his reception room. When he brought them to the door they met others of the bandits making off with the missionary's mules. The chiefs order them returned and went away without doing any harm whatever.

4. Control by means of the contrary expression.

We should also use the method which is more physiological. Our voice, breathing, eyes and muscles should be given an expression contrary to that which anger would impose upon us. We should either remain silent or at least speak deliberately, quietly, and pleasantly. If a cry of hatred or impatience is about to escape through your mouth, breathe deeply two or three times and release the air slowly, and you will extinguish it. Keep the muscles of arms and hands, mouth and face loose and relaxed. Above all make sure that a smile gives the eyes a kindly, gentle expression. And at the same time keep your thoughts on something pleasant.

174] ACHIEVING PEACE OF HEART

After one of my lectures in Rio de Janeiro a lady came up to tell me about her troubles, her bad temper and that of her husband. "My home is a hell," she said. "We are always quarreling, although we pass for good Christians, and even devout ones." I advised that she go look at herself in a mirror and practice smiling with her eyes. "When you have learned how to make this deep and open smile, and when you know that your husband is returning home, make an act of Faith: 'Here comes Jesus Christ disguised in the defects of my husband. He is coming so that I may smile at Him, love Him, and serve Him.'" A month later she came back to thank me for the advice; her home had been transformed. They were happy. She had modified the thought and the external expression of anger.

Anxiety and Phobias

After passing through the fears of childhood we learn, perhaps by experience, about more reasonable grounds for fear. And we protect ourselves against them. Yet oftentimes the environment and our imagination make us see dangers where there really are none, or else magnify our fears a hundred times.

Strong impressions of terror or lively bouts of anxiety and fear, whether they come from conversation, or from a vivid imagination, or the movies, leave something like a residue or sedimentation in the subconscious. This residue is a tendency towards insecurity, or a feeling of anxiety. And when this feeling invades an idle mind it tends to fill it with anxiety images, provoking organic alterations such as physical inhibitions, trembling, contraction of the blood vessels, pallor, panting for breath, palpitations, and so forth. Fear is a monster which dwells in the caverns of the subconscious. The more vague and confused it is, the more it afflicts us. We should drag it out from its hidden lair, look at it face to face, and then we will destroy it.

How to Destroy Anxiety and Phobias

1. *Make them concrete.* We must illuminate those dark caverns. Answer these questions in writing and in detail: "Just what am I afraid of? And why?" When fear or anxiety is made concrete and viewed objectively, it is destroyed.

2. *Reason about them.* "What probabilities are there that this [the thing I fear] will really happen? And even if it does happen, will it really be as disastrous as I fear?"

3. *Face up to them.* "Even supposing that this happens, what then? So what? Are there not others who have gone through similar crises? Haven't they gone on living and become happy? And even if I have to die, so what? Then can't I begin to be more happy in eternity?"

When we imagine the worst possible natural evil that could happen to us and sincerely accept it and so find a human or divine solution for it, we will be victorious over exaggerated fear.

4. Avoid the exciting factors, or rather the alarming ideas which these stimuli arouse in us. Distract

your attention from them by means of concentrating it upon conscious sensations or by deliberately following out a favorite train of thought or, even better,—

5. Deliberately affirm *contrary judgments*, e.g., "There is no special danger. The probability that this will happen is very small. Even if it does happen, the disadvantage would be insignificant, or at least there would come with it several advantages which would far counterbalance it."

6. Deliberately foster *contrary feelings*, e.g., of courage, or security. This is done by the same means by which fear betrayed us, i.e., by intense acts of courage, by vivid remembrances of peaceful moments or places, by actually saying something with a tone of courage or security in the voice.

7. Associate this reliving of past peaceful moments with the circumstances which had been producing anxiety in you. Imagine that you are in control of the situation and that you are speaking in a masterful tone of voice such as in the case of the young man with the pills or the patient with the locust [Chapter IV].

In a Brazilian seminary I met a stammerer who was afraid that he would be unable to go on to the priesthood because of this defect. Face to face with the Rector of the seminary he could not speak two consecutive words. The same thing would happen when with certain of his companions and in certain classes. On the contrary he spoke well whenever he had learned something by memory. Hence it was the feeling of anxiety which was inhibiting his vocal muscles. He was afraid that the Rector would declare him unsuitable for the priesthood. But I helped him to remove this fear by showing him that he could cure himself if he would implant the contrary feelings in his subconscious by the means indicated above. And so I had him link these feelings to the experience which had terrified him most. I had him imagine and then actually say, "I am going to see Father Rector. . . I greet him. . . And all is serene. I am completely at peace and am master of the situation." At first he spoke the last phrase with the same descriptive tone as the first. But I had him repeat it after me with a tone of security. On doing it with all the courage and force of which he was capable, I felt that he was transformed. Three days later the Rector came to thank me for the good done to his seminarians, and he particularly mentioned that the stammerer had been cured.

IN PARTICULAR

Conquer the Feeling of Inferiority

There is a very frequent type of timidity or cowardice which has its origin in a false or exaggerated concept of one's "inferiority." It may come from a conflict whose proportions and consequences are multiplied a hundred-fold by wounded self-love. Or it may come from a real defect or incapacity in one field which you are extending to others while hiding your real talents and good qualities. Or it may be from an irrational panic about "What they will say" or about receiving ridicule.

An investigation of 270 students in a North American university found 240 of them with feelings of frustration or deficiency, physical inability, a not very sympathetic presence, conflicting loves, little aptitude for study or social life, and remorse.

There are students with brilliant compositions in a written examination whom fear of the examiners will disturb and make awkward in an oral examination. Unexperienced orators and poets who have prepared magnificent compositions, at sight of an exacting audience will begin to tremble. They will grow pale, stutter and even forget what they have learned or prepared. Too severe criticism had, after their first trials, cut their wings for life. There are well trained men who after a failure in business or at one job think themselves unsuited for new ventures. And there are people who converse pleasantly and act courteously who one day are caught ill prepared. We see them grow mute, flush when they have to participate in a social event and finally change into misanthropic solitaries. Typists, pianists, children and young people who are extraordinarily gifted in private or within their family circle often seem nonentities in the presence of other people.

This timidity must not be confused with humility, for it sometimes arises from pride. It causes its victim no little suffering from blushing, trembling, palpitations and stammering. These symptoms appear and disappear without apparent cause. They can even bring on lasting phobias or a mental inhibition. When they border on an emotional shock, they weaken or paralyze the muscles. Humility is not depressing. It is truth and raises one up toward God and confidence in Him. Timidity frequently increases pride or is caused by it.

You must war against so widespread an evil. Above all do not cause such a feeling in children or youths by continually reminding them of and exaggerating their defects. They must on the contrary be encouraged and shown their possibilities for progress. Do not even as a joke give a child terror of ghosts, the dead, darkness or animals. This will probably remain active in his subconscious even after he has grown up. As children, says Fosdick, we only feared two things: falling down, and loud noises. Then other fears went on accumulating inside of us. We should cut the thread of them and root them out. "We should take fear out of its hidden hiding place and look at it face to face."

If you find this timidity in yourself calmly examine the thoughts and motives which cause it. Remove exaggerated deductions from your subconsciousness and have trust in yourself. Make an examination of your timidity in writing and show this to your director or mental adviser. You know that there is no reason for being a coward, that all men are equal, that you are superior to most in your own specialty, that there are many mediocre people, that geniuses know how to cover up their deficiencies and show their good qualities. Soak yourself in these ideas. Boil them down into suggestive formulas and frequently repeat them, especially when signs of timidity appear.

With such convictions and suggestions attack the emotional difficulties. Begin with the more easy ones. Take courage at every victory, often repeating, "I am going to win out," "Each time I have more courage," and so forth. Never use negative formulas or conjure up the memory of phobias or symptoms which disturb you. If you say, for instance, "I am not going to blush," "I won't tremble," "I won't stammer," you will produce the very effect you wish to avoid.

Blushing

Those who blush easily and suffer embarrassment from this, in addition to the method indicated on p. 67 ff., should not give importance to so natural and common a phenomenon. For it only indicates modesty and virtue (bad people do not blush). Go ahead *as if* this did not matter to you and take a greater part in the conversation. Pay more attention to what is being said or done. Let this attention fill the field of your consciousness. With no attention given them, the illusions suggested by timidity and caused by blushing will disappear.

One young teacher who blushed and sweated before his students was greatly impressed and cured by the following reasoning process. "If in spite of feeling myself beginning to blush, I go on firmly and energetically without worrying about it, then I am not only not inferior to others but greater and stronger than all of them. For almost anyone else would act like a coward in these circumstances."

As a bodily treatment you are recommended any tonic or strengthener of the nervous system, breathing exercises, sports or any moderate physical exercise. Practice sureness of gaze, not that you should seem to be staring or boldly provocative, or trying to pierce behind a companion's eyes. But practice a gaze which looks easily and dignifiedly at a point between another person's eyes. If you have photophobia (that is, if light bothers you) keep your back to the source of the light or use tinted glasses.

Superiors or directors who treat with timid people will do well not to look at their eyes or forehead or even sit directly in front of them, but toward the side. Thus the timid will be less bashful and more confident. Nor should they be required before special training to perform acts of self-conquest in which a great objective difficulty comes more from timidity or phobias than pride or a lack of mortification.

Orators who experience their breath growing shorter or being choked off just before stepping up onto the speaking platform should breathe deeply for five or ten seconds, emptying their lungs of used air. At the subsequent automatic filling of their lungs with pure air they will begin to speak with a sure voice and will conquer their timidity.

The Supernatural Remedy

For those who have faith the great remedy is a concrete and heroic confidence in God Who can and will aid us. For He commands us "not to fear," not even "those who can kill the body." Their remedy is also confident and persevering prayer which obtains whatever it asks for. "The more you ask for when you pray, believe that you will receive it and it shall be given to you." Here as elsewhere we must avoid timidity. We must not make the future present, for where the future is made present it is disfigured. The only time that exists is now. The past did exist but does no longer; the future may exist, but does not yet. The only two important times, as Catholics acknowledge in the *Hail Mary,* are "now and at the hour of our death."

OUTLINE DIAGRAM

How to Control Feelings

IN GENERAL
- A chaotic force: direct it
- Do not be governed by likes or dislikes, but by reason
- Govern them
  - by lessening their exaggerations
  - making no change merely on their account
  - thinking about the opposite
  - working against the feeling
- Their release
  - useful—in affective conflicts, noble affections
  - useless—impulsive confidences
  - harmful—from passion

IN PARTICULAR
- Dominate anger
  - controlling thoughts
  - thinking about something else, the opposite
  - working "as if …"

FEELING OF INFERIORITY
- Causes
  - failures, defects, criticisms
  - fear of "What they will say"
- Effects
  - suffering, apprehensive fear, embarrassment (blushing), paralysis, irritation
- Remedies
  - preventive
    - not to exaggerate faults
    - not to instill vain fears
  - curative
    - examine the root cause and its path
    - conviction and suggestion of courage
    - attack difficulties by degrees
- Supernatural remedies
  - confidence
  - prayer

X

How to Train the Sexual Instinct

EDUCATION OF THE SEXUAL instinct is especially necessary because the lower level of mental activity is antagonistic to the will, is very strong in this matter and there are very frequent and powerful exterior incitements to vice.

Difficulty from an Erroneous Attitude

Many let themselves be mastered by the sexual instinct because they think it irresistible or because they are ignorant of the hidden force of their will, others because of an erroneous persuasion that resistance can cause illness. Very many yield because they expect to find satisfaction in it. They expect to satisfy that thirst for the happiness which all humans seek. However, they seldom reflect upon the transitory and cheap aspect of disordered sex pleasure. It cannot fulfill the noble and unlimited aspirations of the spiritual soul. But they discredit the experience of innumerable people who are physically or mentally sick because of this vice. They count for nothing the testimony of the medical profession, sentences of judges and warnings of moralists. All of these show the brutal excesses of this instinct once the reins have been loosened by the first concessions.

And on a higher level, they have no suspicion of the deep joys, delicate feelings, mental clearness and agility of pure souls. They forget the abjection and sadness, despair and emptiness of vice, the tormenting remorse of conscience and the threatened punishment of God.

All education should begin with ideas. When these are modified then acts are easily corrected. Then by means of acts the feelings and force of the unconscious are controlled.

IS CHASTITY POSSIBLE AND USEFUL FOR YOUTH?

If chastity were not possible and useful, no one could will it in earnest, not even if it were imposed merely for social convenience. For the instinct is a brutal one and that barricade very weak. Yet nothing is more contrary to science and experience. The great Jewish psychiatrist of Zurich, Dr. Brueler, affirms, *"Whoever recognizes that chastity and continence are possible will hardly have any sexual problems to bother him."* Again, the professors of the faculty of Christiania say, "This faculty of medicine has the honor of making the following declaration: The assertion recently put forth by several persons and repeated in newspapers and public gatherings to the effect that a moral life and perfect continence are bad for the health is something that is completely false according to our experience. *We know of no case of sickness or weakness which we could attribute to perfectly pure and moral conduct.*"

A document unanimously approved by New York doctors and specialists reads as follows: "In view of the spread of venereal diseases, the results of an unfortunate heredity and the moral evil inseparable from an impure life, we doctors of New York and its environs subscribe unanimously to the declaration *that chastity, a pure life for both sexes, is conformed to the best conditions for physical, moral and mental health.*" In the Brussels International Conference on Sexual Prophylaxis 260 members unanimously affirmed the following conclusion: "*It is above all necessary to teach male youth that not only are chastity and continence not harmful, but on the contrary these virtues are to be most highly recommended from a purely medical and hygienic point of view.*" As long ago as its session of March 22, 1917, the Paris Academy of Medicine insisted on the necessity of making known to youth "that chastity is not only possible but also beneficial and to be recommended for health's sake."

Thus we could multiply testimonials from the most eminent doctors of the entire world in order to silence the pseudo-intellectuals or would-be wise men who take pleasure in spreading the opposite idea. And from still another standpoint we know that what God *commands* all men in the Sixth Commandment *cannot* be impossible or harmful to health.

Moreover, the sexual glands, in addition to their external, propagative function, benefit the organism with the production of hormones specific for the sex of the individual. These hormones are necessary for the physiological well-being of the organism.

A SPECIAL DIFFICULTY

Acts against purity at a tender age, from 6 to 11 years, even without knowledge of their malice, frequently throw the lower mental activity out of equilibrium by fixing in the unconscious an abnormal inclination toward pleasure. Or early indulgence may transfer the instinct to the wrong method or sex (sexual inversions), depending on its first realizations. And it leaves a strong tendency to look for comfort, ease and pleasure in everything, and to flee from a hard life, inconvenience and pain.

Wrong satisfactions during puberty engrave this emotional pattern even deeper. And it results in an unconscious tendency to reproduce images and memories of pleasure. Persons or circumstances similar to those met in past indulgence at once arouse sexual thoughts or tendencies and impulses to realize them. The environment—movies, beaches, magazines or pornographic advertising—multiply these incentives until it is extremely difficult to resist passion. This is a difficulty, yes, but not one which it is impossible to conquer.

REMEDIES

Preventive Remedies.—Watch over children lest they learn or practice dangerous acts, urged on by bad companions or the example of immoral movies and pictures. In the case of adolescents who feel the awakening of instinct and are capable of reflection, teach them in private with dignity and clarity the sublime purpose of Providence in the sexual instinct, the possibility and utility of controlling it, and the grave moral obligation not to go beyond its wise norms. We should calm their nascent curiosity and prevent their satisfying it with corrupt companions. We shall then be able to have them elicit that free will act without which all will be lost.

Curative Remedies.—First of all, if erroneous ideas are held these of course must be corrected.

To counteract the unconscious influence of feelings toward pleasure arouse contrary feelings and tendencies by accustoming your body to work, a hard life, mortification and even pain (dignified by Faith), and by withdrawing it from comfort and pleasure. Healthy, vigorous sports are no little aid to this end.

Avoid persons, objects, reading, conversations and spectacles which involve a less pure association of images and tendencies. To will chastity, yet not avoid these incitements, is like setting out to walk on a slippery hill.

When evil tendencies or thoughts appear resist them at the very first moment, "while they are still weak." Do this by opposing other images (conscious sensations, voluntary concentrations, acts which require attention) and other tendencies (wanting to avoid Hell, win Heaven, please Jesus Christ, save souls).

Whenever one very chaste and virtuous young man met friends and relatives of the other sex, he would be disturbed and attracted by impure thoughts without knowing how to avoid them. It was enough to advise him to practice consciously associating other images with the idea of woman—for instance, the excellence of the mother who bears children for Heaven, the Holy Ghost dwelling within her by Grace, the sublimity of the Virgin Mother of God. In a few days he returned to express his gratitude. This new, voluntarily induced association of ideas had done away with the other subconscious and instinctive ones and he felt tranquil and happy.

To attain better resistance avoid lower states of mental activity (alcoholism, romanticism, somnolence, mental vagueness, daydreaming). In these your imagination or subconscious feelings have free rein. And your will and reason are, as it were, asleep. Then the whole man is at the mercy of the first impulse. The first impulse will rise up in a rolling wave, especially if you are also in a too comfortable bodily position. This latter, because of an unconscious association with the sense of touch, awakens the lowest instincts. You will indeed have the power to resist even then, and for this reason will be responsible for your acts. The holy Curé of Ars fled the sensation of comfort as if it were fire.

Against ideas which impel you to perform an impure act, oppose the feeling that you are able to avoid it and the concrete will act of an opposite movement. For example, command your feet not to go into a certain place or your hands to remain crossed on your breast for a definite length of time. Do this in order to strengthen your character, develop your personality, please Our Lady, merit Heaven. (Do nothing "in order to avoid sin," for such a reference will awaken the ideas and impulses which you are trying to control.) Made concrete in this way you can feel these acts as possible and you will really want them.

Once you have done all you humanly can in this very difficult matter you still need recourse to God to obtain supernatural strength by prayer, Confession and Communion. This grace will never be denied you when you seek it with entire humility, confidence and perseverance. The experience of many centuries, by all races and men of every intellectual and social position, demonstrates that these supernatural means do conquer the special difficulty of remaining chaste.[1]

---

[1] Cf. the encyclical of Pius XII on Holy Virginity (*Sacra Virginitas*), Mar. 25, 1954; and the encyclical of Pius XI on Christian Marriage. (*Casti Connubii*) Dec. 31, 1930.

OUTLINE DIAGRAM

How to Train the Sexual Instinct

- **Possibility**
  - Testimony: Dr. Brueler
  - Faculty of Medicine of Christiania
  - Doctors of New York and environs
  - International Conference at Brussels
  - Paris Academy of Medicine
  - God commands it

- **Difficulty**
  - Fixation of inclination toward pleasure because of acts performed
  - Association of ideas and tendencies

- **Remedy**
  - Preventive
    - watch over children
    - instruct adolescents
    - stress acts of the will
  - Curative
    - correct erroneous ideas
    - form positive tendencies and contrary habits
    - avoid incentives
    - resist beginnings with
      - other images
      - other tendencies
    - avoid states of lower mental activity
    - oppose bad impulses with
      - concrete will acts
      - the conviction of triumph
    - prayer, Confession, Communion

XI

How to Be Happy

HAPPINESS IS NOT found but made. It does not depend on what you do not have, but on the use you make of what you do have. It is not something far from yourself but the most intimate part of your being. It is the consciousness of a good, and the greater and more lasting this is, the greater will be your happiness.

You need not travel many lands to find happiness, nor burden yourself with back-breaking labors to win it. It is enough to follow your own road, the road of duty. If you can control your thoughts you will be able to find the flower of joy even among the thorns of suffering.

We all strive for happiness. God wants us to be happy. He repeats it a thousand times in the Scripture and Liturgy. "My peace I leave with you." "Your joy no one will take from you." "Rejoice always in the Lord." "Alleluia." Joy is possible then in all circumstances of life.

However, there are many who do not find it because they go looking for it where it is not to be found, in vice or illicit pleasure. And so upon returning within themselves they find their heart empty and feel tedium, disgust and sadness. They try to forget by means of amusements, movies, parties, novels, and so on. But they do not get rid of the cause of their unhappiness, nor do they give their heart the satisfaction of duty done. They are satisfied with merely hiding their lack of happiness.

"Joy," says Aristotle, "is the accompaniment of a perfect act." Now an act against conscience or duty is essentially vitiated or imperfect. It can then produce, even after some momentary delight, only a deep and lasting sadness. But even those who strive for joy where it may be found sometimes find only suffering, and because of this they drown themselves in a sea of sadness. Yet suffering should not be an obstacle to your joy: The bee draws honey from flowers, and the soul can draw honey from thorns. But this process is patented—in Christianity.

OBJECTIVE SUFFERING

Suffering can be an objective thing; for example, the sickness, poverty or failures which God positively wants you to suffer. It can also be mostly subjective, the effects which the first type produces in you and which you do not control. These effects are sadness, worry and fear which God only permits. Here what He positively wants is your reaction to them, your control of them.

Be happy then "negatively" by overcoming objective suffering. Convert it into joy. How? By shifting your gaze from the unpleasant aspect, from the ugly face of suffering, and concentrating on the bright side. Mentally you have this power, acquired by the re-education of concentration. (See Part I.)

Suffering actually has two sides to it, a pleasant and unpleasant side. The unpleasant side contradicts your tendencies, sensuality, natural inclinations, pride, self-will. Do not fix your attention on this unpleasant side. Suffering has a pleasant side also. In the natural order suffering can be pleasant because it brings an increase of experience, strength, counsel, and patience. But this natural side alone is but small consolation. Hence the difficulty in comforting atheists, but how easy to comfort Christians! Considered in the supernatural order suffering is exceedingly attractive. It is the role which, while on earth, God chose for Himself. It is the livery of Jesus Christ. It is a check which God offers us. If we accept it God signs it and our happiness in Heaven will be proportionate to its value. It is the secret treasure of the Cross, made known to and through the saints. And it is the fruit of devotion to the Heart of Jesus. Supernaturally then we are able to increase this inclination to suffering and find our joy in it. It is integral to Christianity, the apex of virtue, the grandeur of the saints whose joy no human event could disturb.

St. Paul said, "I am filled with joy because of my tribulations." St. Peter recommended, "Be filled with joy in your sufferings." The Apostles "left the tribunal joyfully because they had been judged worthy to suffer insults and sorrow for Jesus Christ."

St. Ignatius Loyola attained complete dominion over his feelings. The doctor forbade him to think about sad things. He examined himself. The saddest of all would be the total destruction of the Society of Jesus. Yet he decided that fifteen minutes of prayer would be enough to reconcile himself even to this.

St. Francis Xavier had such consolation in the Molucca Islands where he suffered so much that he exclaimed, "It is enough, Lord, I shall die of joy."

St. Theresa used to repeat, "Either to suffer or to die." And St. Mary Magdalene de Pazzi used to say, "Not to die, but to suffer!"

On the missions, as a matter of fact, the missionary's greatest consolation after a day of suffering is to repeat before the Tabernacle, "For you, O Lord!"

It is within your power, then, to change objective suffering into joy instead of sorrow.

SUBJECTIVE SORROW

In the face of present or imminent disgrace any normal person first feels a sense of dejection and worry. But by considering its attractive aspect he soon controls these feelings and they do not last very long. However, in sick or nervous people such feelings keep coming back and become obsessions. They produce persistent sadness, phobias, or scruples which destroy all peace and joy. These are crosses which God permits, but which He wants you to control. You must then fight and get control of them.

Control of Subjective Sorrow

1. In addition to the explanations on p. 162, in case of sorrow or internal conflict, *express your feelings externally* in consultation. Make them known as soon as possible to your director or confessor. Tell him of moral acts which burden your conscience, harrowing doubts or indecisions, fears which get control of you. This manifestation with its psychological and supernatural solution will resolve your internal conflict and sorrow.

2. *Live in the present.* The present is a fount of joy. There are delights which crave to be yours. They are external creation (esthetic pleasure) and moral beauty. So give them entrance by attending to the present. You should not think about the sorry past which has already slipped from your hands. Leave it to the mercy of God. And think not on the agony of an uncertain future. Leave this to His Providence. The present is a pleasant path which runs between two chasms, the past and the future. Whoever by sadness or scruples falls into the past, or slips by

worry into the future, ceases advancing toward his happiness.

3. *Live a conscious life.* "*Age quod agis.*" ("Do what you're doing.") If you work on a conscious level, fear, worry and sadness will find no place to torment you. Thus you will lessen and even suppress the influence of a sad and uncontrolled subconscious. "We stand in need of happy people," writes Marden, "who look away from the sinful, bitter and perverse world and turn toward God's world to admire its beauty and perfection."

4. *Practice voluntary concentration on other matters.* These concentrations may be indifferent in relation to those which the unconcious tries to impose on you. If sadness or worry is besieging you, concentrate on some study or occupation that pleases you. Even better, concentrate on something directly opposed. For instance, against fear or disturbance concentrate on living images of peace, control and energy. (See p. 73). In this war you must take the offensive in order to rout the enemy even from his lair in the unconscious.

Cultivate the habit of joy. Your mental make-up is a labyrinthine wood. Your thoughts and acts are men who are tracing a path through it. Where one has passed, the easier it is for the next. So then, if you would win to the heights of joy, you must send joyful thoughts through to open up the trail. Repeat them and reinforce them with acts of satisfaction and optimism until you have enlarged the trail and made it firm through habit. Then almost without noticing it you will find you are always happy.

5. *Practice will acts.* Will the contrary feeling; that is, to be animated, tranquil, kind, happy. Talk and work *as if* you did not feel the opposite feeling (antipathy, worry, fear) or *as if* you were animated, happy, and so forth.

6. *Use suggestion.* At night before falling beneath the dominion of the unconscious and in the morning when leaving its control, think with feeling about images of peace, control and joy. Repeat to yourself, "Everything I do can be a step taken nearer to God," "Every day I am increasing in sanctifying grace," "Every day I am more happy."

7. *Moderate your desires and aspirations.* Keep them within reasonable limits. Seek not for body or soul or anything else a greater security, health or prosperity than God wishes it to have in this world. Thus scruples or worry will lessen or disappear.

8. *Overcome negative and depressing feelings.* Do this by introducing other feelings which are positive, sublime and ennobling, such as love of an ideal, of God, souls, or Heaven. Overcome petty, low and disordered self-love with true love of yourself and your spiritual and eternal good. Before this sublime reality all fears, sadness and phobias fall to earth.

Happiness in this life is not divorced from sacrifice. Our satisfaction increases in the measure that we make those who surround us happy, that we seek the greater glory of God, and in proportion to what we sacrifice to this end.

POSITIVE HAPPINESS

You can have a happiness and joy which is not external and vain but interior, true and well-founded, one which fills your heart with satisfaction. This happiness has four aspects and comes to us through as many channels:

Aesthetic pleasure by which we receive within us the beauty of the external world through conscious sensations, when we contemplate the beauties of nature or of the arts, and especially when we do this in the light and warmth of an ideal. (Cf. Chapter II, pp. 16 and 27; Chapter VI, pp. 94-96; and Chapter XII.)

Intellectual pleasure when by intellectual concentration we possess the truth with certitude, and perfect it or complete it by analysis and synthesis. (Cf. Chapter II, and Chapter VII, pp. 112-114.)

Volitional satisfaction in the power of producing, and in doing, what we value. This type of happiness is the result of exercising a firm and constant will. (Chapters III and VII); and finally,—

Emotional or affective satisfaction at feeling one's own kindness irradiating others, and the kindness of others being diffused in oneself through the elevation and equanimity of our feelings (Chapters IV, IX, and XI).

Your human capital is twofold: your faculties and the time for making them produce. You can have no true satisfaction if you see your capital diminishing each day yet bringing you no return. Nor can you have any satisfaction if you feel your time passing in useless amusements or occupations. You ought not to feel that each passing moment is lost or less profitable. You should feel that it is a source of your own and your neighbor's well-being, and a fruitful seed of an immortal and happy life in Heaven.

To bring about this satisfaction and sense of fulfillment the "life" element should also be present in a vigorous functioning of your intellect and will. Then you will find in your mental concept of happiness the characteristics of unity and totality.

The scholar who makes a discovery has great intellectual pleasure. The mother who is always loving and showing her love for her child is very happy even in the midst of work and sufferings. If that pleasure of the scholar were not disturbed by other ideas and distractions and were prolonged by new and more brilliant findings, and if that of the mother had as its object not a mortal child with all its imperfections but one which would never be separated from her and had all possible good qualities, then we would have true, complete mental happiness. Before it, all merely bodily happiness would grow pale, fade and pass away. You could sum it up in these words: *fulness and unity of your mind and feelings.*

Now let us see how this happiness, though limited in this world, yet unlimited, secure and eternal in the next, is in a real and true sense near at hand. With re-education of control presupposed, apply your understanding to knowing not some small part of the truth but all the truth, infinite truth, truth in itself, God. Each day you can discover new horizons without ever exhausting this infinite fountain of truth and beauty. This is the joy of spiritual persons at receiving in prayer those supernatural lights which we call divine consolations. These eclipse all worldly happiness and cannot even be imagined by those who have not experienced them.

Dedicate your will and feelings to loving the infinitely lovable good, God. Strive to realize that He is not far off from you, but close by in all created things. In these He is at your service and gives you joy. Try to possess Him in the Eucharist, human in body as you yourself. And enjoy a holy intimacy with Him, present as He is within you through Sanctifying Grace.

This is the type of joy in union with God that made a St. Francis of Assisi complain of the sun that it rose too early and forced him to leave the delights of a night with God. Happiness impelled St. Ignatius, when he saw a flower, to say with tears of consolation, "Be silent, be quiet for I understand you." He would remain in ecstatic contemplation of the Divine Beauty of which the flower was but a pale reflection.

Speaking before a Youth Congress of Catholic

Action, one of the leaders said, "At first in prayer I used to look toward Heaven but ever since I realized that God was within me, I look toward myself and feel great joy." Tears came to his eyes and were joined to those of his listeners. He was happy at loving and feeling God within himself. That is why the great mystics who felt the presence of God in this world speak so many marvels about this little-known happiness.

St. John of the Cross insists that the devil admitted to him that if he had a body and if, in order to see God, he would have to climb a pole studded with thorns and needles, he would not hesitate to do this for ten thousand years in exchange for enjoying the sight of God for a single minute.

Some Thoughts on Changing Sorrow into Joy

Passing over the threshing floor the southwest wind raises eddies of dust. But sweeping through flower gardens it raises a cloud of perfumes. So does the wind of suffering act differently in different souls.

The Divine Heart of infinite happiness is "bound with thorns." If you feel the touch of thorns in your heart it is a sign that God is reaching out His heart to you, a sign of the embrace of Infinite Happiness. But happiness will enter into you only through your wounds. God left a trail of blood at His passage through the world; no longer can there be doubt about which is the path to glory, the road to permanent happiness.

Acceptance of sorrow is a contract for work made with God. You agree to construct some great thing with Him. You are the workman who does not see the plans. God is the architect with sublime and magnificent designs.

Nothing great is accomplished without suffering and humiliation, says Newman, and everything is possible by using these means. We must be friendly with suffering. It is a selfless and faithful friend who reminds us of true goods. Souls are instructed by word of mouth but are saved by sacrifice.

Some Thoughts on Happiness and Joy

Happiness is a noble, peaceful and recollected lady who dwells in the hidden fortress of the soul. She knows and tastes its treasures. Frequently she shows herself at the windows of the face and wreathes it with a smile. She clothes the face thus with the brilliance of rational being. This is something about which neither animals nor the most beautiful flowers can boast.

When the polished, peaceful mirror of consciousness reflects a ray of the sun, some good possessed or soon to come, its spontaneous reflection is joy, a smile. If the sun of Infinite Good shines directly upon it, it will reflect happiness.

Life should be a perpetual joy, the joy of living for God, of serving Him in one's neighbor, of saving souls, the austere joy found in suffering. There is the joy of living in a present of infinite value, joy for a past entrusted to the Divine Mercy, joy for a future assured by His Paternal Providence. Have joy in work, and if this is beyond your powers, then have joy in prayer. If even this seems impossible for you, then have joy at least in suffering in Christ and for the sake of Heaven.

The apostle who takes doctrine and example and together with those sows smiles, and then waters these with prayers and sacrifices, will win many souls. "Joy," says St. Paul of the Cross, "is the sun of souls. It enlightens those who possess it and enlivens as many as receive its rays."

The exercise of Christian charity is the best way to make yourself joyful. And this is your most effective contribution to the happiness of others. Smiling eyes scatter more rays of joy than precious diamonds. Through joy you will better perform your duties. And your burdens will be lighter. It will be your consolation in solitude, and your best introduction to society. You will be the more sought after, the more trusted and better appreciated.

The vicious, degenerate or low person may come on the stage of life as a loud and vulgar jester. But he is almost never sincerely happy. Almost never can he wholly forget what weighs upon his conscience. Evil is a cold hand which freezes smiles. But a frank and hearty smile is almost always an indication of a noble and pure heart. The virtue that smiles is the more beautiful, and often the most heroic.

OUTLINE DIAGRAM

How to Be Happy

NECESSITY

- God wants you to be happy { not in vice, nor only in amusements, but in duty, and within you
- Avoid pessimism { contrary to desires, feelings, instincts

ACTIVITY

- *Objective suffering* (accept the disgraces, etc. which God wants you to)
- Cultivate optimism
  - natural { gives experience, strength, counsel
  - supernatural
    - Cross of Christ
    - His role on earth
    - a check drawn on Heaven
    - the great Architect
    - example of the Saints
- *Subjective sorrow* (which depends on you)
  - by expression, confidence, Confession
  - live in the present (aesthetic pleasure)
  - conscious life
  - concentration on joyful things
  - contrary actions and will acts
  - suggestion of peace and joy
  - moderated desires
  - deep emplanting of sublime feelings

POSITIVITY

- Intellectual { a scholar's pleasure at attaining some truth / unlimited joy with all truth
- Affective { a mother's happiness in loving her child / highest happiness in loving and possessing all Goodness

XII

How to Choose an Ideal

A great life is the great dream of youth realized in mature age. Alfred de Vigny

THERE IS A GENERAL or abstract ideal (learning, for example, or art, skill, service, sanctity, patriotism) which can be the goal of your actions. And this goal you can strip in your own mind of all possible defects and adorn with all good qualities. This becomes your particular ideal. The ideal chosen by you becomes the object of a tendency or inclination. It is a detailed picture of your forceful and permanent desire of the more general goal.

THE NATURE OF AN IDEAL

The Intellectual Element

There is especially required, as the very word "ideal" indicates, a great idea (the general ideal).

This is a concrete and constant idea, a goal, a purpose, a good that is precisely, clearly and constantly foreseen. It is a fixed idea, a permanent attention, with all the power of concentration and action which this implies. "Fear the man of a single idea," says an old proverb.

The Feeling Element

Your ideal results in a fixed and instinctive tendency, at the same time sensible and spiritual. You are in a state of forceful impulse toward that good which constantly presents itself as fulfilling the aspirations of your being. It tends to attract related inclinations to itself and its own direction, and to repel opposed ones.

The Will or Executive Element

That permanent attention and feeling influences your will. As a result your will acquires a new force and constancy. And your ideal is then translated into repeated acts. It is axiomatic that a fixed idea and constant tendency impel to action.

FALSE IDEAL OR EVIL PASSION

This too will constantly influence your will, hence its great strength. But it is the desire of an evil which is, by supposition, presented as a good (that is, disordered sexual passion, passion for gambling, intoxication, undue ambition). It does have some good as its object (pleasure, the momentary physical good of some tendency or of one of the senses). And this fixed idea is associated with remembered feelings of pleasure already experienced. It fills the field of consciousness and leaves no room for reflection upon the fact that this momentary partial good of merely one part of your being sometimes leads to sickness, a lasting general illness of the body. Or the pleasure is forbidden because such a false ideal involves moral evil, disease of the soul, sin. It may eventually bring on the physical, final total evil of both soul and body in an eternity of shame.

Evil passion disunites, unbalances you by making you seek a partial good which is incapable of satisfying your instinctive tendency toward your whole good. Hence it will cause you an intimate sense of sorrow, feelings of sadness, restlessness, lack of mental control. Your personality will not be secure, but will find itself wandering astray from the path.

TRUE IDEALS

Effects of a True Ideal

The noble ideal of unity, harmony, vigor and fullness of life increases the physical and mental perfection of your acts. Unity of thought and desire does away with parasite ideas, makes concentration easy, brings pleasure and maximum return to work and study.

A Latin student used to hate this subject and failed it three times. But the ideal of literature and oratory still shone brightly in his mind. So it was easy to make him understand how useful and necessary Latin is to this end. At last the hated subject was overlaid with joyful colors and in his next examination he received a very high rating.

Singleness of thought, as we said in Part One, is not fatiguing. And because it is pleasant, it is conducive to rest. And so the ideal which makes you think steadily of what you most desire is a source of rest and joy. This is the reason, in cases of "overwork," for the effort to discover the patient's interests or ideals in order to help him to rest.

Many energies for your education and perfection are released by the ideal. The ideal of patriotism has made heroes of many timid souls. That of scholarship or research has fostered much constancy and pleasure in overcoming difficulties. The ideal of sanctity or the priesthood, or that of the Christian family, has preserved countless youths unspotted among the sloughs of sensuality.

The ideal of consoling Jesus Christ in His weak or sickly members has aroused and sustained holocausts of self-sacrifice and charity in asylums and hospitals. And the ideal of winning new cities and nations to Him has appealed to adventurous souls ever since the first Pentecost. Saul of Tarsus and Francis Xavier are each a colossus of heroism and superhuman grandeur, the fruits of this ideal. And they lead along behind them thousands of self-sacrificing and valiant missionaries. One aspirant to the apostolate among pagans used to say, "The ideal of my whole life is to sacrifice everything, furrow the seas, suffer everything, save one soul, then die."

As the ideal issues in a permanently vitalizing tendency, it attracts other unopposed inclinations to itself. The contrary ones it annihilates or weakens by leaving no room in the mind for the type of thought or feeling they feed upon. Your happiness increases because of this unity and exuberance of your intellectual and emotional life. You experience the natural joy of perfect acts and the profound satisfaction which follows upon merit and moral goodness.

Ignatius of Loyola fell wounded in the battle of Pamplona. His human, knightly ideal was turned into a divine ideal on contact with the *Lives of the Saints* and the *Life of Christ*. His ideal became "The greater glory of the great King." And his life was transformed into one of marvelous efficiency, unshakable peace and superhuman heroism.

HOW TO CHOOSE YOUR IDEAL

1. Choose an ideal which will not be in conflict with your total good (that is, with your final goal in life), but which will further it and make it easier to attain. Your main purpose in this life is to prepare for the next.

Caesar, Alexander the Great, and Napoleon, each had an ideal of conquest which gave unity and efficiency to their lives. But the good they sought was a partial one and did not satisfy the whole soul.

Moreover, it brought evil upon many peoples and nations, and was barren of happiness. All three have left us their admissions of disillusionment.

Cicero and Demosthenes had the ideal of rising in eloquence to direct their country and correct abuses. This good was ever before their eyes, ever the object of their desire. It made them overcome difficulties, attain great success, and enjoy profound satisfaction. But lower objectives filtered into their ideal, and so it did not fulfill the aspirations of their whole being.

2. Choose an ideal in agreement with your aptitudes and personality.

The Spanish historian, Menéndez Pelayo, considered the black legend spread throughout historical writing about Spanish Catholicism in its "Golden Age." He conceived the ideal of defending his country and religion from such great calumnies. So he studied and surpassed his colleagues in learning and elegance of style. His books astonished the world and he lived an intensely happy life while writing his marvelous *Historia de los Heterodoxas Españoles*. He lived a full life and had a happy death.

3. Let your ideal be found outside of and superior to yourself. Otherwise, you could say with a famous novelist, "Charlie is a little state bounded on the north, east, south and west by Charlie." If your ideal is your body, its boundaries are limited indeed. Corruption and death come in but a few years.

HOW TO CHOOSE AN IDEAL

The ideal of life *is* the development of the whole being for the profit of others and the service of God. It is the transfiguration of our instincts into a higher spiritual love. It is living in oneself and not, as it were, apart from oneself, among others and not apart from them, in God and not apart from him (José Serre).

4. Let your ideal be practical and bring you to act at the present moment on the good thought or noble purpose you have. Do not forget that, as Lemoine puts it, "the most beautiful moment in life, the richest and most significant for the future is the present moment, at the present moment you can amend the past and construct the future." And in the present minute you can glorify the Infinite Being and by saving souls set new jewels in the divine crown of His external glory. You may say that an ideal is not perfect which cannot be realized at every instant. "If I cannot now realize my ideal," says Adela Kann, "at least I want to idealize my reality."

The greatest ideal of life is to realize at every instant the ideal of God, His most holy will. Or put it this way: to feel yourself in all things in harmony with the thought of your Creator. "The ideal of life is to live it fully and with delight," we may say with Jeglot. The ideal is to have a healthy care of one's physical life, an unlimping moral life (duty, justice, truth), a serious and orderly intellectual life, a life of the heart with a twofold movement (giving oneself and guarding oneself). The ideal is above all an intense spiritual life which is at the present moment clear, deep and primarily interior. Then it will later be an apostolic one. And the ideal life should also be joyful, for service, prayer and even suffering should enter into the great joy which is God.

5. Your ideal should be concrete and summed up in a few words to be frequently repeated.

John Berchmans understood the heroism of duty perfectly done even in the smallest affairs. *"Maximus in minimis,"* he would say to himself. "I shall be outstanding in the smallest things." And he reached sanctity at the age of twenty-two. Stanislaus Kostka, hero and saint at eighteen years, made it concrete for himself thus, "I was not born for present things but for the future, for higher things *(ad altiora natus sum)*."

THE IDEAL OF IDEALS

If the infinitely perfect God were to become incarnate, this God-Man would then be the ideal of humanity.

Now it is a fact that the supreme Grandeur, unlimited Goodness, eternal Truth, infinite Beauty, God, was not only made man, our equal, companion and model, but also willed to be the price of our ransom on the Cross, the food of our souls in the Eucharist and our reward in Heaven.

This God-Man, with all the rights of Creator and Redeemer, of excellence, wisdom and goodness, Who wishes to reign over men and Who alone offers them their greatest good in time and eternity, is not only not loved and obeyed by them all, but very many are ignorant of Him, forget and insult Him. And not a few of those who say they are His offend Him or give Him only fragments of their heart, the scraps of their love.

Yet instead of hurling sentence of condemnation He opens His breast, shows you His wounded Heart. With cries of love He says to you, "You, at least, love and console Me, make Me reign." He offers you the consoling pact He made with St. Margaret Mary, "Take care of Me and My affairs and I shall care for you and yours." He will provide for your temporal and eternal good, your health, life, family, business, your soul, its virtues and eternal salvation. He will do this in the measure in which you give Him pleasure and glory. When you ratify this pact all worries, scruples and phobias disappear. Your supreme good is to be taken care of by Another Who understands it better than you do yourself. He wills it Himself and can procure it for you.

Elements of This Ideal

1. Surrender the past to His mercy and the future to His providence in order to live a happy life in the present. Surrender body and soul and everything to Him, for Him to care and provide for according to His will.

2. Take as your one and only ideal for every instant the giving to Him of the greatest possible pleasure

by duty done, charity for your neighbor, the apostolate of souls and fervent prayer. Summarize it thus: "Most loving King, loved and insulted, I wish always to do everything the better to love, console and glorify You."

3. When your heart is freed from other affections, worries and desires, give entire possession of it to "the Heart which loves and is not loved." Enthrone Him in your heart. Make Him absolute and sovereign King of it to console Him for the sharp wound caused by chosen souls who do not receive Him or give Him only a corner of their hearts.

4. Feel His loving Presence in you by sanctifying grace, adore Him, give Him company in this living temple. Above all consult His desires and ask His orders. Let Him reign in your senses, faculties, feelings and works.

Effects of this Ideal

There are wonderful promises made to those truly devoted to His Heart. They will have blessings on all their undertakings, peace, fervor, sanctity, eternal salvation, an effective apostolate.

1. Mentally you will obtain the change of sorrow into joy. You will see suffering as very attractive since the King, Infinite Wisdom, chose suffering for Himself. Crowned with thorns He Himself asks for victims to help Him by voluntary suffering to placate the justice of God and save souls.

2. You will obtain the unification of your life through this sublime ideal. It is an ideal which is realizable at each and every moment. You will overcome that bothersome duality of mental life, phobias, worries and subjective sorrow.

3. You will obtain a consoling fullness of your intellectual and emotional life by knowing, loving and possessing Infinite Truth and Goodness. This will happen in a most attractive and intimate manner, that is, by the God-Man dwelling within you, opening His breast to show you His Heart, impatient with love for you and struck by sorrow when you do not permit Him to give you even greater gifts.

Such a happy person as this, dominated by the interests and person of Him who takes possession of it and reigns completely in its depths, Who communicates to it His own peace, happiness and life, is like the clear, crystal water of a quiet lake. Human events will, like gentle breezes, scarcely trouble the surface of the water and will not disturb the clear image of blue sky, symbol of divine peace and happiness, which are common to both hearts, the throne-heart and the Heart Enthroned.

OUTLINE DIAGRAM

How to Choose an Ideal

TRUE IDEAL
⎧
⎪
⎨
⎪
⎩

False ideal { idea, tendency and will fixed upon evil / this causes turbulence and disunion

Effects { unifies and harmonizes life / gives concentration and efficiency / helps rest and enjoyment / perfects and dignifies

Choice of an ideal { in harmony with your ultimate end / conformed to your aptitudes / outside of and superior to yourself / practicable, realizable at every instant / make it concrete in a few words

Ideal of ideals, Christ the King

object { most noble: the ideal Man / most lovable: Love that is not loved / most useful: that He might reign in all men

concrete { contract, unconditional surrender / He will take care of you / "whatever pleases Him more" / motive: to love and console Him / method: make Him King of your heart and accompany Him, obey Him, identify yourself with Him and His interests

effects { spiritual—His promises { peace, fervor / blessing, salvation / effective production
mental { unification of life / change of sorrow into joy / killing of phobias / consoling fullness of life of { intellect / feelings

XIII

A Short Summary of Advice

(Directives for health and efficiency)

1. Be conscious of your mental and bodily capital. Recognize the limitations of your strength. If this has been depleted by an extraordinary or prolonged effort, know how to replenish it in time by proportionate rest. Do not prolong concentration of attention for more than two hours without a few minutes of conscious sensations and muscular relaxation. The sick, weak and convalescent should abbreviate their effort all the more.

2. Do your job or everyday duty with the greatest possible perfection, that is, with concentration, naturalness and pleasure. Avoid all tension, haste and disgust. Find in your work the strength and joy of an ideal. *"Age quod agis,"* "Do what you're doing."

3. Do not try to realize at the instant *all* the good and greatness to which your impulses urge you, but

only what is possible *at the time* and which a tranquil judgment shows you is proportioned to your abilities.

4. In time of relaxation avoid exaggerated competition. Recognize and accept the physical, intellectual and moral superiority of others. If you must be pre-eminent in something, let it be in goodness, understanding and patience.

5. In time of failure or adversity know how to find and how to reflect on the goodness or usefulness this offers for yourself or others, for time or for eternity. Set this counterweight against excessive sadness and discouragement. Accept the inevitable and base your ideal upon it. This will be the secret of your efficiency and happiness.

6. Avoid the tension which comes from doubt and insecurity about your health, skill, and temporal or eternal success. Trust in your strength and divine aid. Let religious faith and tranquillity of conscience be your guarantee.

7. Make use of the greatest of your faculties by means of deliberate, concrete and motivated decisions. Then put them into execution without fatigue or further discussions. This will give you a strong and healthy personality.

8. Recognize the double tendency in you, the angel and the beast. Make the higher level of life control and rule the lower levels. Make the good of your whole being keep its supremacy over sense-pleasure, caprice or the good of a single part.

Made in the USA
Monee, IL
01 July 2024